Headhunters' Encounter

With God

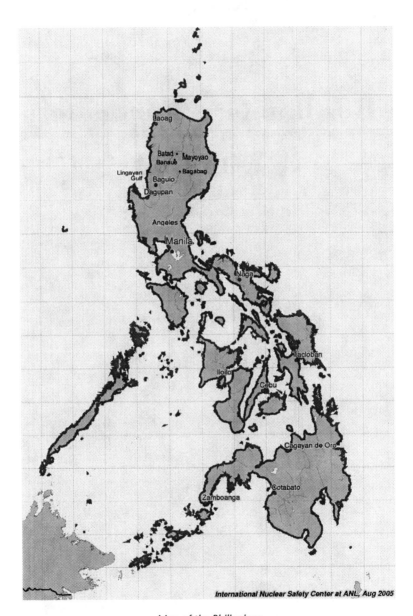

Map of the Philippines

Headhunters' Encounter

With God

An Ifugao Adventure

Len Newell

iUniverse, Inc.

New York Lincoln Shanghai

Headhunters' Encounter With God
An Ifugao Adventure

iUniverse books may be ordered through booksellers or by contacting:

iUniverse
2021 Pine Lake Road, Suite 100
Lincoln, NE 68512
www.iuniverse.com
1-800-Authors (1-800-288-4677)

ISBN-13: 978-0-595-40691-3 (pbk)
ISBN-13: 978-0-595-85055-6 (ebk)
ISBN-10: 0-595-40691-2 (pbk)
ISBN-10: 0-595-85055-3 (ebk)

Printed in the United States of America

In memory of Doreen,
my beloved

How beautiful on the mountains
are the feet of those who bring good news,
who proclaim peace,
who bring good tidings,
who proclaim salvation,
who say to Zion,
"Your God reigns!" (Isaiah 52:7)

CONTENTS

ACKNOWLEDGMENTS

In writing this book, I am especially indebted to four people. Melanie Thomson worked tirelessly in editing the manuscript and suggesting areas for improvement. Andy Bruchmann and Neil Carey worked on photos and a map of the Philippines to make them acceptable for publication. The one to whom I owe the greatest debt of gratitude is my wife Johanna. She was a constant inspiration to me and helped in so many ways that I can only acknowledge her input here in a general way.

The work in which Doreen and I, and later Johanna and I, were engaged was under the auspices and direction of the Summer Institute of Linguistics. Wycliffe Bible Translators, Canada, provided the finances that allowed us to work in Ifugao.

To these two institutions, to the individuals mentioned above, and to many others too numerous to mention, I owe a debt of gratitude for the completion of this book.

INTRODUCTION

The initial chapter of this book begins with an account of the origin of the Ifugao people and how they may have found their way to their homeland in the rugged mountains of north-central Luzon Island of the Philippines from the Lingayen Gulf area on the western coast. Abandoned agricultural terraces, overgrown by forests, can still be found inland from the Lingayen Gulf, along the western slopes of the Cordillera Central mountain range, which gives some credence to this theory. Unfortunately, the historical origins of this remarkable ethnic group have been completely lost in antiquity. Therefore, the account of these beginnings is hypothetical.

I collected the materials used in describing the events involving the anthropologists Conklin and Pittman in chapter 1 during personal interviews of Ifugao people in the village of Hapao. The specific events of this account include reconstructions of what happened. However, I have attempted to make the account as factual as possible.

From chapter 2 through the end of the book, I have related events that happened involving Doreen and me, and later Johanna, as I personally remember them. I have attempted to make them completely factual without embellishments. If there are any departures from facts, they are unintentional and due to memory errors. Direct quotes are, of course, my reconstructions of what was actually said.

All scripture quotations, unless otherwise indicated, are taken from the Holy Bible, New International Version, copyrighted 1973, 1978, and 1984 by International Bible Society. Used by permission of Zondervan. All rights reserved.

1

BEGINNINGS

Bone-weary, the small band of voyagers dragged their frail outrigger boats onto the shore and secured them against the wind, which threatened to drag them back out to sea. They had battled savage storms for weeks. The sails had long since been ripped from their boats, and the voyagers had been blown aimlessly but inevitably eastward at the mercy of the gales, with nothing more than canoe paddles to give faint direction to their course. That each boat had been able to keep track of the others was a tremendous feat, and they attributed it to the help of minor gods among the pantheon of deities they idolized and placated. Their voyage had taken place perhaps around the year 300 BC.

Still somewhat dazed from the relentless reeling and rocking of their boats, they found it difficult to stand on solid ground. They were not seasoned sailors but merely terrace farmers in search of a new land where they could peacefully pursue their agricultural ambitions. They had no idea where they were, but their hopes were strengthened by the seemingly boundless miles of mountains visible through low-hanging clouds. These mountains held promise of a hospitable environment conducive to terrace farming.

This group of people—mostly men, with a few women and children—were Malays and had come from what was later to be known as Indochina. The land from which they had come was overpopulated and held no hope of a future for these desperate souls. Life had consisted of laboring long hours in the fields for rich landlords, with little to show for their efforts. When they were not laboring, they were at war with enemies who constantly sought to take over their territory. Their only hope was to find a new land, and for that purpose they had assembled a small fleet and had set sail along the eastern shore of the Asian mainland well south of China.

They had traveled northward in the hopes of finding a section of mountainous land on which they could establish a new colony. Not far into their journey, a fierce storm blew them completely off course, and before they could recover, other storms developed and completely confused them. Their limited navigational skills only allowed for guidance by the sun during the day and the stars at night. For many weeks they had been adrift on the perilous ocean with neither sun nor stars to guide them. Of the fleet that had begun the journey, only a few boats had survived. They had ended their voyage on the other side of the South China Sea, caught in a little hook now called the Lingayen Gulf. On the west coast of the island of Luzon in the Philippines, Lingayen was not more than eight hundred miles directly across from Indochina. However, they had probably doubled that distance as they wandered aimlessly over that wide expanse of ocean.

These Malays had carefully planned their new life. They had brought with them plants, seeds, chickens, and even pigs for breeding. These supplies would be the meager beginnings of their new colony. Nevertheless, two or three chickens would have to be spared as an offering of thanks. A sacrifice to the gods of the winds and typhoons was essential to ensure that no further calamity would befall them. So, on the sandy shore of Lingayen, the priests among the little band squatted and muttered their multifarious prayers to the unseen spirit world. This task accomplished, they set their faces inland on a new adventure and a new life.

To reach the wooded foothills required only a day's travel, and then the Malays began their climb into the Cordillera Central Mountains. As they pressed inward, they encountered no resistance from the local population, which was made up of nomadic people, pygmies with black skin and kinky black hair, who sparsely populated the territory. As the Malays journeyed, they would only get a fleeting glimpse of these miniature people, who were terrified of them. Upon seeing the Malays, the pygmies immediately retreated farther into the interior.

The pilgrims began to encounter surging streams that creased the mountainsides and tumbled down into the lowlands, where their waters were tamed into a rambling river that flowed to the sea. These streams would provide a source of the water needed to inundate and irrigate terraced slopes. This typography enabled the Malays to terrace the mountainsides and grow rice on the western slopes of the Cordillera mountains. The well-established Asian colony would continue its culture centered around rice agriculture and the worship of animistic beings, including those that had followed them on their fateful pilgrimage.

Old rice terraces are reported to date back to about 200 BC. Some, now completely overgrown by forests, are found on the western slopes of the Central Cordillera mountain range near the Lingayen Gulf.

Priests recite prayers while using a bowl to catch the blood of a chicken being sacrificed. The paraphernalia for sacrificing includes a rice wine jar, brass gongs, and a bowl with rice wine.

As years and eventually centuries passed, it became clear that these mountains were not ideally suited for terrace farming. Frequent drought caused rice fields to dry up, resulting in a shortage of food. Thus, as generations passed, children of previous generations, instead of being satisfied with tilling the fields their fathers had built, abandoned them and resolutely pushed north and east to find and terrace slopes that received more rainfall. Eventually, after several centuries, these people reached a land known today as Ifugao.

It was a rugged land. Spurs and ridges rambled in an aimless maze separated by narrow, treacherous ravines. This land would thoroughly discourage any but the most determined and skilled terrace farmers. By any measure, the task to tame these mountains was daunting. It would be necessary to carve terraces out of the craggy mountainsides with only wooden implements as tools. The farmers would be required to build sturdy stone walls to protect against the erosion of relentless rains year after year. Water from mountain streams had to be diverted through irrigation canals along narrow ledges and into the rice fields. The farmers also constructed huge runoff canals to prevent the collapse of these works of wonder. Their labors were a daring challenge to nature. However, this challenge was exactly what these Malays, later to be known as Ifugaos, were looking for. They set about the task of building what would be known as an "Eighth Wonder of the World"—an awesome task still being tended after hundreds of years.

The Batad Rice Terraces, an "Eighth Wonder of the World." It is estimated that if the Ifugao terraces were placed end to end, they would reach halfway around the earth.

Here the Ifugao people continued to evolve a way of life that they had brought from mainland Asia. Their grasp of technology would eventually rival the most complex cultures of all Southeast Asia. Careful selection of rice seeds and other cultigens continually improved the quality and production of their crops.

Most striking, however, was the evolving religious system. The Malays had brought with them from mainland Asia an understanding that the relief of sickness required the sacrifice of numerous animals, food, and valuable possessions to spirit beings. As years passed, the number and complex organization of their gods—both benevolent and evil—as well as their intimate relationship with them became more and more extensive. They came to believe that calamity and death resulting from fierce tropical storms, earthquakes, or the violence of their enemies, like sickness, did not just happen; there was obviously a spiritual cause.

Such catastrophes indicated that the gods were extremely angry and needed to be appeased with sacrifices much more powerful than just animals. So the practice of offering human heads gradually developed.

But whose heads?

They obviously could not offer the heads of neighbors.

Taking neighbors' heads would require, in retribution, the heads of those seeking to appease the demons, a penalty imposed by village elders. This was a penalty too costly to bear.

So they looked elsewhere.

Descendants of the first immigrants gradually settled in numerous valleys throughout the region. Some groups in different valleys maintained friendly trade relationships with each other. Other groups, however, lost contact with their neighbors over mountain ridges and became enemies. They began to occasionally kill these enemies and soon developed a complicated system of headhunting. Thus began an endless system of killing, head taking, ceremonial sacrificing of heads, and, in response, revenge killings by those who had been raided.

A man relaxes in the doorway of his house. When we arrived in 1954, skulls of sacrificed animals and heads of enemies (pictured above the animal skulls) decorated the outside walls of houses.

Life, such as it was, continued in this way through the ages with no hope of relief. People were born, lived out their short, relatively uneventful lives, and died. It was not until the twentieth century that the Ifugao people received hope of relief from their fear of the spirit world and its oppression.

THE COMING OF "CIVILIZATION"

Locked in the remote northern Philippine mountains, the Ifugao people had little contact with the world outside their borders until the arrival of the Spaniards. In 1565, the Spanish Army along with Spanish Catholic missionaries began to take control of the Philippines and gradually pushed into the interior of Luzon Island. They eventually reached Ifugao—as the Ifugaos' territory is also known—and set up a government office in Kiangan. The Spaniards crisscrossed Ifugao with horse trails in some of the more accessible areas. In 1898, the United States was at war with Spain and took possession of the Philippines.

There were two important results of this colonial occupation. One was that the Americans began building roads into Ifugao, and this hastened contact with the Ifugao people. The second consequence was that public elementary schools, usually through grade six, were built in all the provinces of the Philippines. Great effort, sacrifice, and risk of danger on behalf of Americans and lowlanders resulted in elementary schools being built throughout Ifugao, some in the most remote areas imaginable. However, except in areas where the American government held direct and firm control, it was not possible for schools to be staffed by Ifugao teachers. This was partly because there were few educated Ifugaos.

More importantly, however, was that areas outside of American control—and this included most of the province—were still hostile toward each other and engaged in headhunting. No Ifugao dared enter areas hostile to his or her own home territory, for fear of being beheaded. The American occupational government attempted to control headhunting in remote areas only when they were made aware of heads being taken and made brief forays into these areas. For this reason, teachers from areas bordering the mountain provinces, mostly Ilocano speakers, became the first teachers of Ifugao children.

With the coming of World War II, the Americans lost control of the Philippines, and Japan replaced them as the colonial government throughout the archipelago. The Japanese established themselves in all major centers of Ifugao but were fearful of entering the more remote areas. The result was that the people of these areas reverted to the unrestrained practices before the arrival of any outside governmental control.

One such area spared Japanese occupation was the Batad Valley. Japanese soldiers did not venture into this territory because of its remote ruggedness and the fierceness of its warriors. They did reach the summit overlooking Batad, but here the Ifugao people had built ingenious traps to kill them if they dared venture beyond the summit. Trees, shrubs, and vines were so dense that there were only narrow openings where people in single file could pass. Along these openings hidden spears had been positioned horizontally. Supple green poles were arched backward and, if triggered, would propel a spear at the chest of any unwary Japanese soldier who chose to venture beyond the summit. The Ifugaos also dug and ingeniously disguised huge pits to trap anyone who had escaped the spears and were unfortunate enough to stumble into them. Huge boulders were positioned above these pits and were triggered to fall and crush those who had fallen in. Skulls of Japanese soldiers who fell victim to these traps, along with those of other Ifugao enemies, adorned the outside walls of Batad Ifugao houses long after the war ended.

CONKLIN AND PITMAN LOSE THEIR HEADS

Little was known of the effects of World War II on the Ifugao people. The American Army had chased the Japanese Army into remote Ifugao mountains, and General Yamashita of the Japanese Army had surrendered to General Douglas MacArthur in Hungduan, a village in western Ifugao. Both the American Army and the captured Japanese Army left Ifugao as soon as the war ended.

Shortly after the war ended, two American anthropologists, Conklin and Pitman, decided to find out how the Ifugao people had survived, especially in areas where the last battles were fought. No public transportation was available into Ifugao, and certainly not into the areas they wanted to visit. So they undertook a grueling hike from the province of Ilocos Sur eastward through the southeastern sub-province of Bontoc and on into Ifugao. They were headed for Hungduan, where the Japanese Army had surrendered to MacArthur.

Both men wore backpacks that contained clothing, personal belongings, and blankets, since they intended to camp along the way. Both had long, black beards that, to the people of Ifugao, made them look like beings from another world.

Conklin and Pittman should have understood the absolute necessity of traveling with guides who could speak the local language and explain to the Ifugao people the reason for their visit. Inexplicably, they had no guides. They may have attempted to hire a guide but could find no one brave enough to take on the task.

After all, it had been several years since anyone from the outside world had been in contact with the people through whose villages these men intended to pass.

Conklin and Pittman's adventure started with a rugged, two-day hike through southern Bontoc into Ifugao. The first two nights they slept under the stars and enjoyed the quietness of being alone—or so they thought. They entered Ifugao early on the third day. They were surrounded by an eerie sense of solitude. Not a single Ifugao met them along the way. This seemed strange, but their apprehension was mitigated by the assumption that they were passing through largely uninhabited territory. What they did not know was that as soon as they had crossed into Ifugao, they had been observed and followed. Ifugao men are experts in stealthily tracking wild game without making a sound. Thus, it was easy for them to follow these two men from some strange world. The Ifugao men wanted to determine the reason for this intrusion into their territory.

As shadows lengthened and night came on, the two visitors were in the Hapao Valley among beautiful Ifugao terraces only a few kilometers from the village of Hungduan, their destination. Still they saw no one. Signs of life, however, were everywhere. They observed broken terraces under repair. Stones in one pile and soil in another were ready to be put in place. Irrigation dikes were partially cleared, indicating that men had been at work that day and had gone home with their work only partially completed. But not a single soul was seen.

Houses situated among terraces are used as rice granaries in which rice is stored and paraphernalia, including rice gods, are kept for sacrificing when storing or retrieving rice.

As these two men discussed where to find a sleeping place that night, they came upon a small, elevated house built on stilts in the midst of the Hapao terraces. The house was well kept, but it seemed no one lived there. They had a choice to make. They could go on into the village of Hapao and, provided someone could speak English, announce their presence, or they could stay the night in this little one-room house and enter the village the next morning. They chose the latter plan.

They put down their backpacks, kicked off their boots, and prepared to make themselves at home, completely unaware that Hapao warriors were nearby, observing their every move. They kindled a little fire, boiled some water, and made coffee to perk up their cold food rations.

Weary from a long day's hike, they climbed up into the house to spend the night. They were somewhat surprised to see the contents. In one corner was a pile of rice sheaves. On the floor they observed two black carvings, a male figure and a female figure, along with a rice wine jar. They were beginning to realize that they had entered a rice granary that contained not only rice but objects used in sacrificing to spirits. Little did they realize—though it should have been obvious—that this was a sacred granary, forbidden to be entered by any but a priest who would ceremonially open it for storing or removing grain. The unsuspecting men were soon asleep.

Two rice gods, a priest's ceremonial hat on top of a rice basket, a priest's ceremonial backpack, a spear, an altar box, a bowl with rice wine and spoon, and a pile of bones and dried parts of sacrificed animals.

The Ifugao people of Hapao were furious. Who were these suspicious men, and why did they have no respect for something as sacred as a rice granary? This required a village meeting to determine what should be done. First, who were they? Certainly they were not American soldiers. Many of the Hapao people had seen Americans during the close of the war. The black beards of these men were puzzling and possibly portended an ominous future event. A rumor had reached Hapao that another powerful nation was opposing the Americans. They were Russians, so perhaps these men were spies of this powerful country, scoping out the land in preparation for another war.

Some thought that these two men should be roused to try to find out their purpose in passing through Ifugao. They would, of course, have to be severely punished for desecrating a sacred rice granary. But who could talk to them? Certainly no one spoke the language of these foreigners, nor did any of the Ifugao know enough English to possibly interpret what the men might say. As the discussion continued, it became clear that there was only one sensible thing to do. These two men must be beheaded! This would put an end to the uncertainty, and the heads could be used to appease malevolent spirits. It might even be that the Philippine and American governments would reward them for their decisive actions.

So, without further ado, the Ifugao men who had tracked the two foreigners went with other village leaders to the sacred rice granary.

"*Pumitaw ayu!*" they shouted. "Come out!"

Two unfortunate, sleepy men appeared at the doorway. They were dragged outside and quickly dispatched, with no attempt to communicate with them. With the anthropologists' heads taken, the Hapao people performed a centuries-old ceremony to appease the spirits who controlled violent death. This was the end of Conklin and Pitman.

By this time the American government was in the process of regaining control of the Philippine countryside. Retribution was swift. Many of the Hapao men were arrested, tried, and convicted of murder. Eight years later, I hiked into Hapao from Banaue, one of the larger towns along the Ifugao roadway, and talked with some of the people involved in this most unfortunate event. It was obviously a sad case of mistaken identity by a people not in tune with what was going on in the outside "civilized" world.

2

IFUGAO ENTRY

A CALL TO IFUGAO

Professor Otley Beyer, an American educator, came to Manila soon after the Americans took over the Philippines. His first assignment was to Banaue, in northwestern Ifugao, where he functioned as supervisor for the Banaue district of the Bureau of Public Schools. While in Banaue, he married an Ifugao woman and learned much of the culture and language of the Ifugao people during his stay. Upon retiring, he had established a private book museum in Manila where he functioned as curator. The museum contained, along with a few physical remnants of Philippine history, an impressive collection of most of the writings on the various known tribal groups in the Philippines at that time. Most of these books were anthropological and linguistic descriptions of these people, along with a few dictionaries and word lists of their languages.

During 1953, our first year in the Philippines, I often visited this museum to research information on various smaller indigenous Philippine groups and spent hours talking to Professor Beyer about the Philippines.

One day he said to me, "I'm going to Ifugao for a few days, and if you would like to go, I would be happy for you to come along."

I was delighted. This would be my first opportunity to get out of Manila to an area where I could meet Filipinos who were completely different than those who lived in the big city.

During a three-day stay in Banaue, I got my first introduction to Ifugao life. We visited clusters of small Ifugao houses with skulls of water buffalo arranged on the outside walls. There were bundles tucked up under the eaves. We were told that these bundles were the bones of the ancestral dead. In all of the time we were there, not once did I see evidence that the Gospel had reached this place. Here were a people for whom Christ had died, but they were completely without a witness to that fact. From what Professor Beyer told me, they had no part of the word of God.

We returned to Manila, but it was impossible for me to get the plight of these people out of my mind. I shared my concern for the Ifugao people with my partner and wife, Doreen.

Doreen and I had known each other from the time we were teenagers in Canada. Doreen's determination, as mine, was to serve abroad in some capacity as a missionary. Part of my training for my missionary career included the study of linguistics and translation theory, and I had set my path toward linguistics and translation on some foreign field. We were drawn together as lovers with a common interest. We were anxious to marry and work as a team, and although Doreen felt that she would probably never be a linguist, she was confident that she could work with me as a linguistic and translation helper. We were married in 1950, and in response to an appeal for linguists to work among the preliterate groups in the Philippines, Doreen and I volunteered to go there.

Doreen and I arrived in the Philippines in 1953. During our first year in Manila, we had been earnestly searching for a group of people who were in need of what we hoped we could offer. Now we determined that if God allowed, Ifugao would be where we would serve him in our linguistic and translation ministry. That desire became a reality the next year.

THE DEDICATION OF ESTHER

I doggedly followed my guide up the steep, rocky mountain. I knew then why this northern province of the Philippines had been named Mountain Province. It was 1954, and my mission that day was to find a place where Doreen and I could live to begin our Ifugao work. At the mountaintop, at the edge of the little village of Gohang, we stopped while I gasped and panted to get my breath. As we looked back across the valley and at the mountains rising on the other side, the sight that met our eyes was breathtaking. There, like a giant stairway reaching heavenward, the famous Ifugao rice terraces stretched from the river in the deep valley gorge hundreds of feet up to almost the top of the mountains and as far as the eye could see in both directions. It staggered the imagination to realize that these terrace walls, if placed end to end, would reach halfway around the earth, and that all of this had been accomplished by a so-called primitive people using nothing but crude wooden shovels over a period of some two thousand years.

Through the centuries since Christ's presence on earth, countless thousands of people had labored and sweat in these same fields. It was almost unbelievable that every last one at the close of life had gone out into the blackness of death alone, not once having heard the name of the one who loved them and wanted to be their Father. Surely after waiting so long these people deserved to have the precious message, the book that could guide them in their endless search for the way to peace in this life and in the afterlife. We were determined, if God willed, to give it to them.

My guide, all the while, had been talking in a strange staccato speech to a young lad in a loincloth. At the end of the discussion, he announced that a sacrifice to spirits and ancestors would be taking place shortly. The sacrifice was for the protection, health, and successful life of a baby girl only eight days old. We could observe what was going on if we wished. I did not need a second invitation to agree to observe the ceremony.

We entered the main living area of the house of the baby's family. There was virtually no furniture, and the walls were bare. In the middle of the floor, there was a large carved wooden communal bowl filled with rice brew. Near the bowl stood an ornate jar about twenty inches high, which I later learned contained rice wine, or more accurately, rice beer. It had been brewed from a mixture of roasted rice grains and homemade yeast. A small altar box lay open and contained blackened chicken bones, betel nut, dried betel leaf, and one or two other objects that I couldn't identify.

Surrounding these objects, seated cross-legged on the floor, were the baby's father, two Ifugao priests dressed in their traditional red and purple robes, and a couple of other men, who I assumed were less important priests. Outside this circle lay three or four chickens that would be sacrificed. Numerous men and women lined the walls of the room, either squatting or sitting on the floor. We joined this group to observe what was happening.

Each priest dipped a little saucer made of a coconut shell into the communal bowl filled with the home-brewed beer. They were chanting prayers in an ancient language used only for their rituals, much of which not even the other Ifugao people could understand.

One at a time, the chickens were killed, and as each life fluttered away, the two priests with glassy stares prayed for unseen deities to receive the chicken's spirit, and in return, bless and protect the child. Finally a squealing pig, its feet securely tied, was brought in and, by plunging a sharp stick immediately behind its front leg and into the heart, it too became a blood sacrifice to the animistic gods.

If only these people could have had a chance to read the beautiful words of scripture:

"[God] did not want animal sacrifices ... for sin. What God wants is for us to be made holy by the sacrifice of the body of Jesus Christ once for all." (Hebrews 10:8, 10 New Living Translation)

They must have the word! Then the full force of the task that lay before us became crystal clear. Surely this was the corner of God's vineyard that he was calling us to. What a tremendous and fearful task he was entrusting into our hands!

Dr. Esther Aguinaldo, whom I dedicated to the service of God and her people in 1954

The sacrifices and prayers were finished, and proudly the mother produced the object of the whole occasion—a darling, brown-skinned little Ifugao girl. Quite timidly, the father, who had seen more of civilization than most of his fellow tribesmen and was able to speak a little English, approached me.

"Would you please baptize my daughter and make her a Christian?" he begged.

With the help of my guide as interpreter, I explained that I was not a clergyman and that it was not my custom to baptize babies. However, if they liked, I would pray for her to my God who was above all gods. To this, the father readily agreed. With the precious young life in my arms, I bowed my head and prayed that God would take this child and lead her to know him at an early age. The father asked me to name her, so I gave her a good Bible name. I announced that she should be called Esther, and I prayed that, like Esther of the Bible, she would be used by God to bless her people.

A month later, Doreen and I came to live in Ifugao with our one-year-old son. In fact, we were able to acquire a little house in the village of Gohang, only some three kilometers from Banaue, a major Ifugao market center. This house was next door to the house of Esther's family. Money, though scarce, was used to buy staples such as salt and sugar, so the owner was happy when we offered to pay him a little monthly remuneration for being able to live in his house. We lived and worked there for the next three years.

In 1958 it was time to leave Ifugao and the Philippines for a speaking tour in Canada and study program in the United States. I had studied four years of theology at a Bible college and had received a diploma in that field. I wanted a bachelor's degree so that, at a later date, I could go on to an advanced study program in linguistics and anthropology. Most of our time in America was spent at Seattle Pacific University, where I earned a degree in sociology. Upon our return to Ifugao two years later, following my study program, we didn't return to Esther's village but settled in a more remote area. We lost contact with her family, but years later discovered that because I had dedicated her to God, her father had insisted that Esther grow up a Christian. She went to a Christian high school, completed medical school, and eventually became a fine pediatrician. She has spent much time in Ifugao tending to the needs of her people, particularly to the needs of expectant mothers and babies.

GIVE ME THIS MOUNTAIN

Again I stood at the foot of a mountain. I was again in search of a place where our family could live and continue our Ifugao work. This time the mountain separated the world of jeeps, trucks, and a semblance of "modern" life from Batad, a mystic land representing life lost in the antiquity of a past age. I had a vague feeling that we were on the threshold of a new adventure, but just what that might entail I had no idea.

During our first stay in Ifugao, Doreen and I had lived along a roadway in Gohang, near Banaue, our market town. The people where we lived had contact with the outside world via lowland merchants coming to Banaue to stock local stores with dry goods. Some local inhabitants had also traveled to the lowland areas. They returned with tales of the wonders of electricity, radios, water coming from man-made iron pipes, and a host of other marvels that kept them up around campfires into the early hours of the morning. There, in a place that seemed like the end of the world, we had learned a little of this complicated language and had experienced the joys along with the frustrations and fears of living with a people still practicing animistic rituals that, among other things, involved headhunting practices.

However, since our initial arrival, missionaries from another agency had come with the intention of "planting churches" in the area, including the village where we had lived. So, having just finished our stay in North America, we decided that this would be a good time to transfer to a place so isolated that it would not gain the interest or attention of missionaries who required the mobility of roadways and motor vehicles. We wanted to follow the example of the Apostle Paul, who said, "It has always been my ambition to preach the gospel where Christ was not known, so that I would not be building on someone else's foundation" (Romans 15:20). Not that we would be *preaching* the Gospel. Our hope was that our neighbors would hear the written Gospel, read it as we translated it into the Ifugao language, and would respond to that message.

We suspected that Batad was such a place. Not only was it on the other side of a mountain over which not even the most rugged land vehicle could pass, but it could not be reached by even a motorcycle or bicycle. It was a hinterland of unknown size and population density. As far as was known, no foreigner from outside the Philippines had ever visited that valley. There were vague rumors that people of the area were still engaged in the practice of lopping off people's heads. We knew that they were animists worshipping—or, perhaps more accurately, appeasing—spirits and demons of all sorts, as well as engaging in the worship and appeasement of their ancestors. This we knew because the practice was wide-spread throughout the accessible regions of Ifugao. Beyond this we could only speculate.

The Batad people had remained for the most part undisturbed in this valley for centuries. They had worked out a social, religious, and economic system that had allowed them to live in this most hostile environment. Were we now coming to upset their peaceful existence? Why did we presume that we had anything that would improve their way of life? We knew that the ways of the country of our origin held out very little promise of a better life for such people. Although we didn't fully comprehend the true significance of why we were there, we understood that the most significant and truly valuable gift that we could bring from our world was God's holy word, the Bible. If we could leave that behind, per-haps—just perhaps—it would make a significant impact on their lives and culture.

We had temporarily established ourselves along the roadway at Dalican, the last village before ascending the mountain to Batad. There I left behind Doreen and our children, Gordon and Kathy, and hiked into Batad alone with a guide provided by the District Supervisor of Schools in Banaue.

The mountain rose before me a mighty challenge, shimmering in the heat of the noonday sun. It wasn't so much the challenge of climbing it that caused my apprehension. I knew that I had the physical strength to do that, or I was pretty sure I did. It was, however, the overwhelming realization that if my family and I were to come and live on the other side of this mountain to do our work, we would have to climb it again and again, month after month, year after wearying year. This mountain stood between the outside world and a people on the inside known as the Batad Ifugao. They lived almost like cliff dwellers, clinging to pre-cipitous slopes. Already God had kindled in our hearts a strong desire to translate his word for them. Yet we wondered if we could tolerate the endless physical challenge before us.

That mountain loomed as a formidable barrier before us! What of the unknown physical dangers? Even more, what of the mental and spiritual battles to be fought if we were really to break through to a people whose language was foreign to us and who we vaguely knew worshipped gods of wood and stone? Could we meet such an awesome challenge? Were we being realistic? The fear of failure weighed heavily upon me.

My guide sat quietly in the shade of a spreading mahogany tree, resting before our assault on the mountain. I stood beside him with silence ringing in my ears. A bee exploring giant sunflowers zigzagged by through the still air. The cool, clean scent of mountain pine was everywhere. I was intoxicated by the serenity and freshness of it all. Standing there, trying to take it all in, I was overwhelmed with a feeling of Divine presence. In my mind's eye, I was taken back to a century in the distant past when an old warrior stood at the edge of a hilly country. His name was Caleb. He was one of the spies who had been sent into a hostile land to find out if God would give the land to his chosen people. While the hearts of his companions had failed them out of fear of the terrifying obstacles, Caleb was overwhelmed by the conviction that God would allow his servants to claim that mountainous land for his glory and as his country. Forty years later when God's people finally entered the land, Caleb still clung to that conviction.

Standing before Joshua, he pleaded, "Give me this mountain" (Joshua 14:12, King James Version).

We all have our mountains. Some are towering ramparts that seem impossible to conquer. Others are annoying little hills that threaten to wear us down. Big or small, though, they are there to challenge us to expand our faith. God invites us to pray Caleb's prayer, "Lord, give me this mountain." God delights to answer that prayer of faith, as he answered mine that day in a way that would have overwhelmed me had I been able to look ahead and see the thousands of precious Ifugao souls that he would claim through his translated word. Caleb's words were on my lips, and as I gazed upward to the summit of that mountain, I prayed Caleb's prayer: "Lord, give me this mountain." With that, I took a deep breath, and with my guide leading the way, began the laborious climb to the pass.

Our climb took us along a path that wound upward through open grassland. Higher up, the path cut a narrow ribbon along a steep slope of shale and presently plunged into the lush greenery of a subtropical forest, which threatened to overcome it. We welcomed the delicious freshness of the cool shade. At one point, our path was interrupted by a thin silver waterfall tumbling from the rocks above into a little pool fringed with luxuriant ferns and blooming pink begonias. The beauty of God's unspoiled nature was truly breathtaking. I washed the perspiration off my face, took a refreshing drink from the stream, and rested before the final ascent.

Later, as I broke out of the forest with chest heaving, I took huge gulps of air to satisfy my starving lungs in the rare atmosphere of the summit. My guide had hiked before me with little more effort than that required of a young man taking a casual Sunday afternoon stroll. The torture of the climb was richly repaid by the majestic view. I stood there with the world of Ifugao, and beyond, stretching out before me. The mountains rose up in high relief, ridge after majestic ridge, like frozen billows poised to break on the rugged, barren foothills that receded into an azure haze of nothingness.

This was Ifugao! This was the land I had waited so many years to see, ever since my first realization of God's claim upon my life for foreign service. This was the home of the people God had called Doreen and me to reach with his translated word. Again, the enormity of the task overwhelmed me.

The mountain on the other side fell away in an awesome sweep, ending miles below in a canyon. On the sides of the mountain were a number of grass-roofed huts that seemed to have popped out like mushrooms after a spring rain. In these huts, clinging to these slopes, I knew, lived a people who had never even heard of Christ. I could imagine myself mastering the language of these Batad people and perhaps even understanding their culture sufficiently to talk to them intelligently about Christ's claim on their lives. This, however, was only one of hundreds of other valleys just like it. I was almost dizzy with the realization that behind each of those countless ridges lived people just like the people of Batad. Or were they the same? Perhaps their languages were different from the one I had journeyed here to learn. I had no way of knowing. And who would reach them? Certainly I knew that it was physically impossible to think that I could. The reality of it all overwhelmed me.

Then I thought, *This is my small part of the worldwide work of translating the Bible.* In inaccessible places in the remotest parts of the world are countless people speaking perhaps as many as three thousand different languages. How are they to be reached? Who will go to end their isolation from the Gospel of Jesus Christ by giving them God's word? The answer did not come to me that day. What eventually did happen in Ifugao, I could not, in my wildest dreams, imagine. Only later, as I witnessed God's miraculous plan unfold in Ifugao did I begin to understand his worldwide plan to reach every tongue. I could not reach all these Ifugao people myself, but other servants of God could; he had laid a missionary burden on their hearts, and the native Ifugao missionaries could carry the translated word to every nook and cranny of the rugged country.

The light softened as the shadows of the mountain gradually crept down to engulf the valley, leaving only the opposite side of the valley golden against a retreating sun. We began our descent, quickening our pace. Our encounter with the village of Batad was about to begin.

OUR FIRST BATAD ENCOUNTER

The Batad terraces were dramatic in the extreme. Against the backdrop of Mount Amuyao, they completely dominated the landscape, demanding the admiration of those who viewed them. They formed what looked like giant rows of seats in an enormous amphitheater, beginning hundreds of feet above us and sweeping thousands of feet below. We could only begin to imagine the Herculean effort that had produced these terraces over the course of centuries. Bringing water down from sources high in the mountains and distributing it into a vast array of terraces demonstrated superb hydraulic skill of the Ifugao people.

Two deep channels, running from the mountaintop to as far as we could see below, divided the terraces into three sections. Later, we discovered that these were canals for runoff water. They began as relatively small channels at the top and gradually increased in size as they flowed downward to become huge waterways fully eight feet across and equally as deep. The canals were needed to control the tons of water that were dumped onto these fields during storms and typhoons. Without these channels, the terraces would quickly collapse and slide down the mountainside. The system of terrace water control and moving earth by running water in disposing of the earth in digging these ditches was an engineering marvel to rival that of the most advanced civilization. Yet it was accomplished by a so-called "primitive society" without the benefit of modern mathematics or machinery. My admiration for the achievements of the Ifugao people increased with each new discovery.

Notwithstanding its physical beauty, however, Batad was a wretched and uninviting place. As we hiked down into the first housing cluster, I could see that the houses themselves were miserable little shelters with single rooms no more than eight or ten square feet. The windowless walls were four or five feet tall, and supported the pyramidal roofs. The tiny doorways were perhaps four feet tall. Each structure was elevated about five feet above the ground by four foundation posts, each topped with a disk to prevent the entry of rats.

People sat on logs or squatted on their haunches Ifugao-style, legs firmly planted slightly apart, resting solidly on the calves of their legs. They stared at me as though I was some kind of otherworldly oddity, which I suppose I was. The expressions on their faces betrayed more hostility than interest. It was, I thought, as though I was a canine walking into an alley full of felines … or was it the other way around? I felt the hair on the back of my neck rise in response to that silent antipathy—the enmity of closed minds toward all that is strange or new. As the intruder, I knew it would be my responsibility to provide the means for breaking down this wall of resistance toward someone from outside the Batad world.

The Philippine government had established a small, one-room school for children in this village and a little shack for the teacher. Both had grass roofs and grass walls held together by arrow-grass canes. They had little window openings with wooden shutters which, when closed, allowed no light to enter. My guide took me to the shack and introduced me to the teacher. He was an Ifugao from the market town of Banaue. I explained that I was scouting around to find a place where my wife, our two children, and I could live and work, and he offered to help me as much as he was able. It seemed to me that if I were to make friendly contact with these people, it would probably be through him.

Doreen and I had decided that we would attempt to live in Batad, but there were no houses available to rent. The Ifugao houses were completely unsatisfactory for what we wanted to do with paper and pencil, books and typewriter. So we needed to find a place to build a small house. There were a few empty terrace spaces in Batad, but the moment we began negotiating with the owners, ten or more others would protest, claiming an interest in the property through their ancestral line. After several tries, it was obvious that the lack of uncontested space within any of the hamlets simply didn't allow us to build there.

Finally, at the urging of the Batad schoolteacher, and with the approval of the Bureau of Public Schools, we decided to level a piece of the mountainside that belonged to the public school. This was a daunting task, but the Ifugao men were eager to do it for pay. So began the work of building a wall for the terrace that would provide a little ledge for our house.

BUILDING OUR BATAD HOUSE

It was a wild, stormy morning. I awoke to the sounds of the little shack murmuring and moaning in the unrelenting grip of a typhoon. I was staying in the hut of the Batad schoolteacher to supervise the leveling of a site and building of our house. Would this meager dwelling soon scatter to pieces over the landscape? I had secured my bedroom window shutter the night before, but these furious forces of nature were still finding their way through the cracks of the wood and thatch. Staggering to the front door in the darkness, I opened it to a blast that drove me back into the room. Outside, the day was dark and full of the roar of driving rain. Surely we could not work today. Wrong!

The Batad men were in the process of doing what they knew best—building a terrace wall on the steep mountainside where our house was to be built. Twenty-five strong, the men had been engaged in three tasks. One group of five men was busy quarrying stones from a rocky bank about a half-kilometer away. A second group was constructing a wall using the quarried stones, and a third group was cutting down the mountainside above and throwing the soil behind the stone wall as fill. As the wall was built up, an almost vertical bank above it was cut down. Eventually the two groups would meet on the flat surface of a terrace, the inner portion consisting of solid mountain soil and the outer portion of hard-packed fill tamped firmly behind the wall.

This was my fourth day in Batad. I was staying with Derano, the local elementary school teacher, the only "outside" Ifugao living in this village. Derano and I quickly ate a cold breakfast of leftover mountain rice and dried fish. Starting a fire, even indoors, on a day like this was out of the question. Donning a raincoat, and with my head down against the wind-driven rain, I hurried up the mountainside to the terrace site. There were the workers, in nothing but loincloths, with rivulets of water running down their black hair and over their bronzed bodies. For all the world they looked like drenched rats barely surviving this world of water, but they were working hard.

The men on the wall had almost exhausted their supply of stones and, while waiting for more, began to help move the soil that the men above were digging out. But the soil had turned into a mountain of mud. This soggy mess made work extremely difficult. The futility of continuing in this tempestuous rampage of nature seemed obvious. I tried to communicate with as much of the Ifugao language as I could muster, and used my hands to pantomime what I could not say.

"Men, let's wait out this storm. That will allow the men quarrying stones to catch up so you will have stones to continue building the wall and somewhere to put this mountain of soil. In this typhoon, you are creating mud and making your work doubly difficult."

One of the older men stepped forward.

"*Muntamu ami!*" (We will work!) he declared simply and firmly, with a ring of finality in his voice. He was short in stature, about five feet tall, with a stern, drawn, leathery face and work-worn hands from a life of grueling toil on these terraces during uncounted seasons of both scorching heat and chilling rain and wind. They had no alternate source of money, and I knew how desperate they were not to allow this opportunity to escape them. I tried again.

"Look, men, when the weather clears, the job of building this terrace will still be here, and you will be the ones to work. Let's go home now and wait for the weather to clear." Sullenly and reluctantly, the man who spoke stepped back. I had the distinct impression that he was unhappy with my decision. We were barely communicating, and it seemed that he had just given up trying. The unhappy group picked up their tools and spears and slowly dispersed. Alone, I retreated down to the schoolteacher's shack to wait out the storm. By this time, Derano had gone off some distance to his teaching duties in another little hut that served as the local schoolhouse.

Alone in the darkness of the shuttered shack, a small kerosene bottle with a rag wick was my only source of light. To keep the feeble little flame alight, I positioned myself between it and the most obvious source of wind and rain seeping in. Holding my book to the light, I tried to read. However, the distraction from the howling storm made reading almost impossible.

Then I became aware of another noise. A high-pitched and menacing sound permeated the little shack. Above the tumult of the storm, I thought I could hear words—someone yelling—though I could make out nothing of what was being said.

With difficulty, I opened the door of the shack, and there stood the man who had contested my decision not to work. It was an awesome sight. With one hand, he menacingly waved a bolo, and with the other he gesticulated wildly. His countenance was empurpled with rage, and his words came fast and furious and mostly unintelligible. Nevertheless, the gist of what he was shouting in Ifugao was clear.

"You will never live here! I will drive you from this place!" There followed a succession of venomous speech, the meaning of which, mercifully, I could hardly decipher.

I was dumbstruck! What had I done to cause this tragic misunderstanding? The torrent of hateful epithets continued unabated until, finally, not knowing how else to end this tirade, I cautiously backed into the shack and secured the door as best I could. The cacophony created by my angry visitor gradually abated until there remained only the howling noise of wind and rain.

The wait for Derano's return from his classes was long and lonely. Perhaps he would have some understanding or word of advice that would help resolve this situation. When he arrived, I wasted no time explaining as best I could what had happened. His face was grave and appeared to reflect my own puzzlement. Obviously someone had told him something about it. He knew that the man was Mannong, and he knew where he lived. Weakly, I thought, he tried to play down the seriousness of what had happened.

"It's probably just some small thing that he will get over quickly," Derano suggested. "Let's wait overnight, and then we'll go down into Mannong's hamlet in the morning and talk with him. By that time he'll be calmed down, and I'm sure we can settle this misunderstanding."

I slept little that night. I lay awake praying and listening to the typhoon as it continued to exert its force, though by then with less intensity. Alone in the darkness, with only a wall of grass and reeds to shelter me from whatever was outside, I began to imagine ominous and outlandish possibilities. The one foremost in my mind was that of Mannong stealthily creeping up in the blackness to thrust his spear through the weak and unprotected wall. There would be precious little to stop that spear. I knew that these imaginings were foolish—or at least I hoped they were—but try as I might to dwell on more lofty thoughts, my mind continually returned to that possibility.

As soon as the light of day allowed, Derano and I scrambled down the treacherous and slippery slope of the mountainside to the housing cluster where Mannong lived. In some places the little path widened so that one could descend unaided, but in others it narrowed ridiculously to tiny, well-worn toeholds in the sheer rock. I could only negotiate these dizzying heights with Derano's help. We stepped over the half-gate into a flagstone-paved yard with three houses. A couple dozen people who lived there and in nearby houses had assembled to witness this confrontation.

Mannong was there, too. As soon as he spotted me, he was transformed again into what seemed to me to be a savage and uncontrolled madman. His bolo belt was beside him. With furious purpose, he tied it on with his bolo in its sheath and grabbed his spear. Then, without warning, he charged me, spear pointing forward. I staggered back in disbelief. This could not be happening! Yet it was. Would this bizarre spectacle end my missionary career in such a sudden and senseless way?

However, just when I thought all was lost, four muscular men came flying out from among the crowd, grabbed Mannong, and held him firmly. It was a standoff. Mannong was straining forward, shouting wildly into my face, while I quailed before him.

"He won't hurt you! He won't hurt you!" one of the four men holding him loudly and, I thought, ridiculously assured.

"What do you mean, he won't hurt me?" I responded incredulously. "He's trying to kill me!" If it hadn't been so tragic, this crazy scene would have been hilarious. It was ludicrous in the extreme. With the four men still firmly holding Mannong, Derano and I along with a few others quickly retreated back up the mountainside. So much for Derano's diplomacy.

I was completely bewildered. I had no plan, no sensible scenario with which to extricate myself from this horrible predicament.

I simply said to those standing somberly around me, "I'm going back over the mountain to Dalican. If a miracle happens and somehow Mannong can be placated, we'll consider coming back. If not, we'll have to go somewhere else. We simply can't live in a village where someone is hostile to our presence." I really had no hope that he would change his mind after this terrible and extreme challenge. So I gathered up my few possessions and prepared to leave.

"You can't go alone," they cautioned. "We'll hike with you to the summit."

I wasn't fully aware of the danger then, but Ifugaos had been known to waylay their enemies along the forested trails. With such dense vegetation above the trail, it would have been singularly easy to hide and jump down on an unsuspecting traveler. Even Japanese soldiers during the Second World War hadn't ventured into this mountain stronghold. So with one stalwart Ifugao before me with spear in hand, another one behind, and a few others, our pathetic little group made its way back up the mountain in the rain. We passed through sweet potato fields and into the forest to the mountain ridge. I looked back down into the valley, wondering if this would be the last time I would view this fair but fearsome place.

In Dalican, I related to Doreen the events of the past days. We could do nothing but pray and wait, and that we did. That night, with my wife at my side and the comfort of a warm bed, I felt somewhat more secure. However, confusion and utter uncertainty still taunted me. The following morning dawned heavily overcast. The rain was still falling, and the small, temporary shelter that we called home was loud with the sound of water drumming upon the tin roof, cascading from gutters, and splashing into the inch-deep lake that had replaced the dusty path and bare, parched yard of the previous week.

We were in the midst of breakfast when a knock came at our door. I opened it to find standing before me Derano, along with Mannong, hat in hand and obviously transformed into a meek and mild-mannered man. It was like a vision too good to be true. But there they were, soaking wet, with bits of forest foliage still clinging to them. Derano grinned.

"Mannong has something he wants to say to you," he announced.

"I have come here," Mannong began, "to ask your forgiveness. I was completely out of line yesterday. I want you to come back to Batad, and I will do whatever I can to make your stay safe."

I wanted to dance for joy! I wanted to shout "Hallelujah!" I ended up shaking his hand and hugging him, both completely un-Ifugao things to do. Mannong seemed to understand, and his crusty face wrinkled in a grin from ear to ear as he realized that he had been totally forgiven. Dealing with my blunders would have to wait until I began to better understand the intricacies of this culture and could more fluently express myself in Ifugao.

How it happened I have no idea, but upon our entry into Batad when our house was finished, the people announced that we had been adopted into an Ifugao family. Mannong was our father and Bahhin, his wife, our mother. Truly a miracle! They named Doreen "Kuyappi," and I received the name "Bulayungan," or "Bullay," as a nickname. Bulayungan had been an ancient Ifugao hero from Kiangan in eastern Ifugao.

A few weeks later, when it was necessary for me to leave Ifugao for a quick trip to the United States, Mannong became the constant protector of Doreen and our two children, Gordon and Kathy.

The terrace was level and ready for the construction of our house to begin. Ifugao houses have a much different function than ours. They are not actually lived in. They are built on stilt piles, and they provide a sleeping place and a retreat from stormy weather. Otherwise, people eat, cook, live, and do household chores under their houses. We carefully considered living in two or three of these houses, but with typewriters, paper, and office work to occupy much of our time, we decided to build a modified, simple Western-style building. No Batad Ifugao could build such a house, so we found a carpenter from the market town of Banaue who agreed to come in and build a house for us.

First, though, we needed materials. Far away, in another mountain area, there was a sawmill that prepared pine lumber for house building. It would be a long way to haul this material by truck, and it would have to be carried over the mountain from Dalican to Batad on the shoulders and heads of our future Batad neighbors. There was nothing closer to be had, so we arranged for two truckloads to be delivered to Dalican. When it arrived, we had one load dumped in the village along the roadway just below the shack where we were temporarily staying, and the other load dumped a kilometer down the road where the trail took off up the mountainside toward Batad.

We calculated that it would be possible for them to carry in the entire load dumped at the foot of the trail that first day while we stood watch. The second load—or what was left of it in Dalican—could be carried in on the second day. We hoped our plan would alleviate at least some of the theft from the load left overnight. One Ifugao man whom we had befriended was to receive and list the boards in Batad and check off each carrier. We had little hope of accuracy, but perhaps this would be a deterrent for any who might be tempted not to deliver their loads to the building site. We hiked down to the foot of the trail, and the fun began.

Already about a hundred people were swarming over the pile of lumber selecting pieces to carry. There were stalwart men and women, children as young as eight or ten, and old folks, some of whom seemed too weak to get over the mountain themselves, let alone carry lumber.

"Wait!" I shouted above the tumult of animated arguments as each person vied for the pieces he or she wanted. "We need to list each piece and who is carrying it. The boards you carry will be checked off in Batad." This procedure was calculated to help assure the safe arrival of each piece. In hindsight, my naïveté was laughable in the extreme! To begin with, I could no more control this mob to get an accurate count than I could name and number ants swarming over an anthill. There were also other challenges that at that point I had not even contemplated.

As they broke away from the crowd with their prizes, I was able to intercept a few and list their names, but most slipped away with no record at all of who they were or what they were carrying. Although faces were unfamiliar and tended not to appear distinctive in ways that I could clearly distinguish, as the day wore on I eventually became aware that the same faces were reappearing far too frequently. What was going on? Perhaps they were giving their lumber to someone else to carry in and were returning for second loads. Finally, by midafternoon, we were down to perhaps a hundred boards scattered around at the foot of the trail. I began to notice that no one was picking up these boards, and in fact, few people were at the pile at all.

Then it dawned on me. They didn't want to carry these boards. The remaining pieces were green and wet and so heavy that no one wanted to carry them, especially with an entire load in Dalican waiting to be selected. The load in Dalican! That's where the others must be!

I ran the one kilometer back up the hill, and there they were, swarming over the second pile.

"You can't take these yet," I pointed out. "You haven't finished carrying the first load."

They protested.

"Those boards are too heavy. We won't carry them."

We were at a stalemate.

We sat, looking at each other, as time passed. I could offer more money for carrying the lumber at the foot of the trail. However, we had decided that the most equitable and the only practical way to pay was by each board foot, not by the pound. In the end, they resolved the problem themselves by deciding that they would divide up the heavy lumber and each one would carry his or her share. So the carrying continued.

As the last boards were being carried in on the second day, I followed the carriers to Batad. As we left the open fields and continued the climb into the forest, I almost fainted by what I saw. There, behind almost every tree, hardly hidden from the sight of anyone hiking, were the makings of our house! I knew these people were hungry for money, but this was ridiculous! They were so anxious to carry and get paid for as many boards as possible, that they had deposited their loads in various convenient places along the trail and hastened back to claim their share of what was left. They could carry their loads into Batad later at their convenience.

What could we do about this impossible situation? I mulled this over as we hiked along, and by the time we reached Batad, I realized that it was completely out of our hands. If any percentage of the lumber arrived at the building site in Batad, I was sure that it would be because of the intervention of the Lord. To make matters worse, our Ifugao friend who was assigned to monitor incoming carriers and their boards as they arrived in Batad had been no more successful than we. Again I had woefully miscalculated.

I did not yet know that the Batad people were scrupulously honest. Within two days, all the lumber was at the construction site and accounted for—every stick of it! So the building of our house began.

While I worked in Batad with the carpenter and his helpers, I began building simple tables, a kitchen counter, and cupboards from plywood that had come with the lumber. Not only did the carpenter build our single-walled house, but he also built an outhouse and a shed for our generator, which would be used to power our two-way radio to keep us in touch with our Manila office. The two-way radio was vitally important since we were entirely isolated from law enforcement agencies and any medical help.

The mountainside where our house was being built was completely without water, since there was no nearby spring. Every drop of irrigation water was needed to keep the terraces inundated year-round, and our neighbors guarded their water rights religiously. We would need to collect water from our tin roof in drums, and if this supply failed, we would need to have it carried from a spring about a half-kilometer away. Our supplies, including clothing, dishes, and work materials, were packed in four metal drums that we had brought from Canada. The carpenter built a platform under a gable at the back of our house for our drums. Garden hoses connected the drums and brought water into our kitchen by gravity flow, and I had put in a simple kitchen sink with a water faucet.

Work on our house proceeded apace with little interruption except for one. Doreen, who was in Dalican, kept sending over boxes of our supplies, and I had precious little space where I could store them.

"Please tell her," I urged the Batad carriers who went daily to Dalican to bring in our supplies, "that I have no place yet to put our things. Tell her to wait until the house is almost finished before sending more supplies."

They readily agreed to pass on this message, but supplies continued to arrive. Finally, I hiked out over the mountain myself, only to discover that Doreen was being told to please pack up all of our things because I wanted them in Batad. Again they had found a way to outsmart us and ensure that they, not their neighbors, would be the ones to carry our belongings.

CREATURE COMFORTS

Batad was our home. We had resolved not to build a house at our translation center located just outside of Ifugao. We wanted to be sure that we would not succumb to the temptation of spending much of our time in the relative luxury of a Western-style community where we would have good food and fellowship and would be able to worship regularly with people who shared our faith. This, we reasoned, would distract us from our primary goal of thoroughly knowing, interacting with, and influencing our Ifugao family and friends. Thus we built a home in Batad to accomplish these goals. Gordon and Kathy each had a bedroom; we had a living room separate from our kitchen and eating area. Doreen and I each had a study. Our rattan furniture was comfortable, allowing us to live in relative ease.

Before gaining entry into Batad, we had lived temporarily in Dalican along the roadway. Our house there provided us with a place where we could temporarily store our belongings, establish a supply link with the outside, and plan and execute our entry into Batad.

Our little house in Dalican had a kerosene refrigerator, a luxury item, which we expected to return to Manila when we moved into our new Batad home. We would not have it in Batad. No one could carry our heavy refrigerator five kilometers over a twelve-hundred-foot pass!

Our Ifugao friends, though, had different ideas. Long before we had our belongings carried in, they had taken note of what we had and, in their minds, had decided what each person would carry. Four men came to us.

"We will be the ones to carry in your refrigerator," they announced.

We could not believe that they were serious.

"Oh," I replied, "you do not know how heavy that is. You could not carry that all the way over the mountain into Batad."

They smiled tolerantly.

"We can carry that, and we will be the ones."

I was still unconvinced.

"Well, when the time comes, you can see how heavy it is. If you really can do it without banging it against the rocks, you can be the ones to carry it in."

They grinned from ear to ear in happy anticipation of a tidy reward. We were paying by the pound.

When the day came to actually test their ability, they came with a long pole and yards and yards of stout vine from the forest. The refrigerator was wrapped in blankets to protect it from scratches. They laid it down, lashed the pole to it, and walked off with it, two men in front and two men behind in single file. When it arrived in Batad, there wasn't a dent or a scratch on it. Our estimate of their carrying ability went up exponentially.

The refrigerator was a wonderful luxury. With it, we could bring in meat from the outside and store it in the freezer compartment to be rationed out over the next several weeks.

It proved to have a couple of other valuable uses, as well. Many of the women had upland sweet potato fields far above and beyond us on the mountainsides. They would come home in late afternoons, dirty and dusty from digging in their dry fields, bent over from using little hand trowels all day. They were tired and thirsty. Our porch, which they passed on their way home, had a bench built on both sides, allowing several people to sit and rest. They chewed betel nut, talked and enjoyed a glass of cold water from our refrigerator. It did not take them long to appreciate the ice and the delicious ice water that we served them. Most of them had never seen ice before, and this truly was a miracle.

We also came to realize that the use of ice was the best and most effective way to treat snakebites.

*A betel nut is cut open, wrapped in a betel (pepper) leaf, and put in the
mouth. Lime from a lime tube is added. This mixture, when chewed,
produces a stimulating drug absorbed through membranes in the mouth.
Spent betel masticatory and red juice are spit out.*

Another luxury was our pool. A little stream of water ran down a crease in the mountainside between our house and the nearby hamlet of Hu'ab. The stream ran through luxuriant trees and foliage, and at one spot it widened out over a smooth rock area in the form of a basin before continuing to tumble downward. I looked at that spot and thought, *This would be an excellent place to dam up the stream and make a swimming pool.*

I discussed the possibility with Bubbud and Bon'og. They were young married Batad men who worked with us on our linguistic and translation projects and helped us in many other areas of our lives among the Batad people. They agreed that it would be relatively easy to build a holding dam in front of the downward flow of the stream at the lower end of the sheet rock. After all, building walls is what Ifugao men do best.

So, with a little effort, these two men, along with a half dozen or so of our close neighbors, built a swimming pool that was somewhat round and about twenty feet in diameter. We built a little change room and, for safety, we built a fence with a gate around the pool. This would keep small children from wandering into the pool without the supervision of an older person. It was great. We came, especially on weekends, to have a picnic and swim. How refreshing it was, especially in the dry season, to temper the remorseless heat with a swim in our pool. Our neighbors enjoyed it, too. When we were not swimming, young and old would come and enjoy a swim especially after a hard day's work.

Despite our precautions, however, there was a dark side to our pool. On one occasion, when we were away, some children were swimming. One young girl dove in and failed to surface. The others waited along the bank for her to come to the top, but she remained at the bottom and drowned. It was one of the most distressing happenings of our stay in Batad. In such a circumstance, parents could lose control and strike out against the one responsible for the situation. We were afraid they might blame us for their daughter's death. So, upon our return to Batad, we hurried to their home to comfort them and tell them how sorry we were.

"This is a sad day for all of us," the father lamented. We embraced and cried together over the precious daughter they had lost.

CHARGE!

Our house sat on a little ledge at the entrance to the village. It was a two-story building with living space generally on the second floor and workspace below. Extending from the front door on the second floor was a porch some eight feet wide and twelve feet long. It ridged a gap, allowing us to walk out onto the main trail, which ran past our house. From the porch, we could look down on people below or observe those traveling up the path either to their sweet potato fields above or over the mountain to the outside world. It quickly became a good place where we could have social interaction with our neighbors or do our best to minister to their physical and nonphysical needs.

For us, a favorite pastime after work was relaxing on our porch and greeting people coming home from the fields with their heavy loads of garden produce. They would often stop, get a glass of water from our refrigerator, and share the latest news of the village. We sometimes weighed both carriers and loads to see how much they normally carried, and we were amazed that often the loads weighed half again as much as the carriers. Visiting with them on our porch was a wonderful way not only for us to keep abreast of what was going on in the village but to practice our Ifugao language skills with our neighbors.

Gordon and Kathy also liked to use our porch for socializing, but this sometimes got them into trouble.

Mani was a young married man who was considered rich by Ifugao standards because he owned many of the beautiful terraced fields. He was, however, somewhat irresponsible and squandered much of his wealth on an unhealthy lifestyle. People in general, including our children, did not take him too seriously.

Mani's appearance would have struck fear into any child who was not accustomed to the physique and dress of most of the men in Batad. Of moderate build, he had bronze skin that glistened in the sunshine and rippling muscles from laboriously working and hiking outdoors in the harsh terrain. He was naked to the waist and wore a narrow loincloth. Around his waist, he wore a belt decorated with ocean shells, and a scabbard hung from it to hold his bolo. In his hand, he carried a spear. Our children saw Mani not as a fierce warrior but as a friendly, though careless, neighbor on whom they could play a little prank.

One day, Gordon and Kathy saw Mani coming up the trail. Standing on our front porch, they dropped pebbles onto his head as he passed, then ducked out of sight before he could look up.

Mani looked up, spotted them, and made a mad dash toward them, spear pointed. Both children dashed for the safety of our house. Kathy was the quickest, and, before Gordon realized what was happening, she had dashed inside, slammed shut the door, and bolted it, leaving Gordon outside. He cowered in mortal fear, believing that his end had come. He waited for the inevitable. Mani rushed up.

"What are you doing?" he demanded.

Gordon's reply was little more than a squeaky wail.

"*Bo'on ha"in, hi Kati! Bo'on ha"in, hi Kati!*" (Not me, it was Kathy! Not me, it was Kathy!)

Leaning on the shaft of his spear, Mani spent the next several minutes lecturing Gordon on how he should respect his elders. Then he continued his hike up the trail.

SHARING THE LOAD

Most of our supplies had already been carried in to our Batad home, but I had not brought in most of our books because until shelves could be built we had little storage space for them. In Manila we had packed the books in two fifty-five-gallon steel drums with lids that clamped on. They were extremely heavy—about four hundred pounds each. A trucking company was assigned to bring them north. Word had just come to us that they had now been delivered to Dalican.

We collapsed cardboard cartons that had been used to bring in other supplies and prepared them to be carried out with us. We planned to divide up the books and carry them in, box by box. Early the following morning, several Ifugao men and I set out for Dalican. As we climbed, the morning star gradually faded against the pearl gray of early dawn, draining the darkness to reveal sweet potato fields clinging tenaciously to the mountainsides interspersed with scattered boulders and occasional bushes. As we reached the summit, morning broke in a wash of pale yellow behind the dark and jagged line of the eastern mountains.

I paused in breathless awe to view the stark beauty of this craggy landscape. It was truly God's country. The scenery, however, was entirely wasted on my friends, who urged me to press on toward our goal.

We hiked down the narrow trail and eventually emerged from the dense and luxuriant forest on the Dalican side. There, far below, we could see two faint figures on the trail. As we came closer, it appeared that they were struggling with some very heavy object. It gradually dawned on me that these were our Batad neighbors attempting to carry one of the four-hundred-pound barrels full of books up the mountainside and down into Batad! "Carry" was hardly the word to describe what they were doing. Their procedure was ingenious. The drum of books was lashed with vines in a horizontal position to a stout pole that projected beyond the drum at both ends. Each man held a vertical pole with a V at the top into which the horizontal pole had been inserted, with great effort, no doubt. With a "one, two, three, heave," the men, with shoulders at either end of the horizontal pole, would lift the load momentarily, stagger a short step forward and upward, and thrust the vertical poles again under the load. This process was repeated again and again in a determined effort to reach Batad. Obviously they had hiked out in the middle of the night to be sure that they would be the ones to carry in at least half the shipment of books.

My companions and I were enjoying the coolness of the early morning, but these two were not! Their exhausting labor had turned their brown faces to a rusty red, and rivulets of perspiration streamed down their foreheads and cheeks.

"*Maphod an mahoyang*," I greeted them cheerily in my best Ifugao. "Good morning. We have come to rescue you from this impossible load you are attempting to carry. We have cartons here, and you can repack your load into these."

They would have none of it.

"We will just be the ones to carry this," they retorted. They were afraid that if the load was divided into cartons, others would take some of it, and they would not get all the money that they so desperately craved. So we left them to struggle upward as we continued on to Dalican for the books in the second drum.

On our way back with cartons of books, we overtook them near the summit, where they were still counting and struggling. They did eventually reach Batad that afternoon and, although completely exhausted, were overjoyed by the handsome payment for a load that would ordinarily have required four or more strong men to carry.

GNAWING NOISES

Doreen and I were learning to feel at home and relax in a community that was beyond the immediate reach of law and order of the outside government. Although we were still uncertain how we were being received, we were confident that we were developing a measure of acceptance by a few of the more congenial members of the community. We were beginning to relax during the day as we went about our activities, but we were still experiencing a degree of uneasiness at night. Night noises were especially troublesome.

One night after the last of our belongings had been moved in, we lay in our bed trying to sleep. We were disturbed by a muffled gnawing noise. After listening to this for a while, I got up and tried to identify where it was coming from. Yet as soon as my feet touched the floor, the sound stopped. This was repeated several times, and each time I became more frustrated. It seemed that the sound was coming from our bedroom closet, but it was piled completely full of boxes and clothing that had not yet been put away. The last thing I wanted to do in the middle of the night was unpack an entire closet. However, whatever was making this disturbance was so persistent that in the end, we knew we had no alternative. We brought out box after box and carefully unpacked and repacked, but we found nothing.

Finally, after the last box had been investigated, all that remained in the closet was a pile of clothing. One by one, the articles of clothing were brought out and examined. We were down to a couple of shirts and a pair of boots. I picked up a shirt and then I saw it! A tiny mouse! With lightning speed—but not quite quickly enough to avoid detection—it disappeared into a boot.

"Aha!" I exclaimed as I clamped the boot top shut. "I've got you!" Without the slightest pity for this unfortunate rodent, I shook it down into the toe, and the little creature met its end by my hammer. With great satisfaction and relief, I shook it out onto the floor, and we slept peacefully that night.

THINGS THAT GO BUMP IN THE NIGHT

I do not consider myself to be particularly superstitious. In fact, I have devoted many years of my life to gaining an education in sociology, linguistics, and anthropology, and I hold diplomas and degrees from four institutions of higher learning; I would like to think that my natural inclination is to objectively explain events that on the surface seem to be supernatural. Yet, events in Ifugao have often stretched my ability to maintain my objectivity.

I have never been particularly afraid of the dark or of spooky places. I remember investigating a "haunted" house as a child with my younger brother and some close friends. This uninhabited house had stood in an isolated area for as long as I could remember. We heard scary stories about how it was haunted, so one afternoon we decided we would investigate for ourselves the truthfulness of this report. We silently crept up to the house as bravely and silently as we possibly could. We cautiously looked inside and saw a rope hanging partway down from the ceiling.

"A hangman's noose!" someone yelled. With shrieks and wild shouts, we staggered back and ran as fast as our legs could carry us to get away from that fearsome place. Yet deep down within me I didn't believe it. I suspected that it was just something left over by the last person who had worked inside that room.

However, now I was a grown man in a foreign country. We had come to live in an area where, to be sure, few people of our background had ever lived. We were beyond the immediate reach of any kind of police or other protection, shut away with people who lived as much in the spirit world as in the physical, everyday world around us. I was quite sure I could handle that and could act as protector of my wife, who was as brave as I.

We were, however, not prepared to cope with what we experienced our first few nights in Batad. To understand our plight, it is necessary to imagine what it would be like living away from family and friends or anyone else of our own kind. Our house was located in a rather lonely spot with no other houses nearby. We had just arrived in Batad, so we really didn't know what to expect. Nights were very dark with no illuminating electricity. The night was so quiet that we could hear ringing in our ears.

We went to bed one night, and as we lay in our bed with nothing but a flashlight on a nightstand to provide emergency light, we heard a faint noise that interrupted the stillness. It was a whirring sound. It began on a low note and gradually elevated to a high pitch. This repeated continually. We had no idea what it might be. We had no electronic equipment that might be the source of this disturbance, but we were confident that there was some natural explanation. So we ignored the noise as best we could and went to sleep.

The following night the whirring noise was back, but this time it was interspersed with a clicking sound. I decided that it was time to take action. I got out of bed with my flashlight to investigate, and immediately the sounds stopped. As soon as I lay down, the sounds began again. We sat up in bed to try to determine where the sounds were coming from. They definitely seemed to be coming from within our bedroom. This was foolish. It was stupid, and I was angry. Yet I was helpless to do anything about it. We spent the rest of the night trying to sleep the best we could.

By the end of the week, there were not only whirring and clicking sounds but pings, thuds, and thumps. Doreen and I were both thoroughly exhausted. We could not go on this way. I tried again to locate the whirring sound. This time it didn't stop when I got up. I pointed the light from my flashlight in the direction of the source and quietly approached it only to have it shift to another location in the room. This continued until I was completely frustrated.

I threw myself onto the bed and wanted to cry. Had we come to this place only to be mocked and defeated by silly things that go bump in the night?

It was Doreen's turn to offer a solution to our problem.

"Don't you think it might be good for us to pray about this? It might be that Satan is using these noises to drive us from Batad. If the Lord wants us here, he can surely stop these noises and allow us to get some rest."

Of course he could. Yet, until now, I was unwilling to admit that these were anything but noises that could be explained as natural happenings. We prayed, and the noises stopped and never returned in all the time we spent in Batad. No one has ever suggested to us an explanation of these noises. However, whatever they were, they too were under the controlling power of the one who had sent us to Batad.

RICE WINE AND HOSPITALITY

Back in Canada, our religious teaching forbade us from touching, let alone drinking, alcoholic beverages. So when we arrived in the Philippines, we were ill prepared for a radically different custom, which was especially practiced in the north where we lived. There, the mark of hospitality and friendliness is to offer rice wine to the visitor, and the mark of cordiality and a peaceful intent on the part of the visitor is to accept it.

Before I had time to really think through this cultural clash, I was confronted with a situation in which I had to make an immediate decision. Soon after arriving in Gohang, where we lived during our first stay in Ifugao, I had gone out of my way to cultivate the friendship of Aliguyun, an old native priest. He was a kind, gentle man and would undoubtedly be a true friend and an invaluable source of the Ifugao language and culture. I was very anxious to get to know him well. One day I had the opportunity to visit him in his home. He was dressed in a loincloth with a red and blue robe covering his shoulders and most of his body. The first thing he did was bring out his rice wine in a beautiful Ming jar and a glass for us to drink from.

I was perplexed. Although I knew little of Ifugao custom at that time, I had a sense that this was something important to Aliguyun. I could neither refuse nor accept his offer of specially brewed wine. I wanted to fade into the background and just disappear. However, I could not, so I spent the next several minutes explaining to him as best I could, with a very limited vocabulary and much gesticulation, why my religion forbade me from drinking with him.

As I spoke, I could see Aliguyun's face growing increasingly more serious. Then, all of a sudden, it brightened. Gesticulating, he wanted me to understand that he had the answer. I could come under the blanket with him so that my God could not see, and then we could drink rice wine together. Sadly, I had to tell him that my God could see right through that blanket! With that Aliguyun gave up. We continued to be friends, but I had the distinct impression that we were not as close as we could have been if I could have just brought myself to taste his wine.

In Batad, as in Gohang, an item high on the priority list of our accomplishments was getting to know our neighbors. We were becoming acquainted with those who lived nearby. However, we also wanted to get to know others who lived in more distant villages and hamlets, so I determined to go out into the villages to see them. Many times, as I walked alone, I would experience a rather uncomfortable happening. Walking on crooked trails that snaked around constant bends, I would spot someone coming toward me in the distance, only to find an empty trail when I arrived at where they should have been. Obviously they had seen me, too, and had left the trail to hide in the dense forest until I passed. At other times I would enter a hamlet that I hadn't visited before only to find it completely empty. Clearly, someone had sounded the alarm that the foreigner was coming, and everyone, including babies, had vanished into thin air.

The only remedy was to take a respected elder of Batad with me on these visits. Who better than my father, Mannong? He agreed to go with me to introduce me to these more distant neighbors. This proved to be a useful decision, except for one problem. Drinking rice wine was still a major problem for me, and I had not yet resolved it in my mind. I really did not know how to resolve this problem.

But luckily for me, Mannong gladly fulfilled the custom for me. At each cluster of houses we visited, inevitably the rice wine came out, and Mannong would drink the wine, always remarking that it was a very tasty brew. Unfortunately, this can only be repeated a few times until the imbiber becomes so incapacitated that he cannot go on. I could not persuade Mannong that he need not drink the whole glass each time. Thus, on many occasions, I made my way home alone. In any event, we did get to know our neighbors, even in rather remote areas, and eventually we were completely accepted as true Batad residents.

A SPIRIT'S REQUEST

During those early weeks and months, we were still attempting to sort out fact from fantasy and dependability from delusion and deception. In the context of trying earnestly not to be judgmental of vastly different values, and struggling to gain acceptance, we did our best to be helpful, to be accommodating, and not to offend.

One evening two men came to our door with a strange request.

"We would like to borrow your wife's necklace." That seemed a harmless, although strange, request.

"Her necklace?" I asked. Doreen did indeed have a couple of necklaces but had never worn them in Batad. How did they even know that she had one?

"Yes. You see," explained one of the men, "my baby daughter is gravely ill. We are having a sacrifice to a spirit to cure her sickness, and it is asking for your wife's necklace."

The spirit had been quite definite about what it wanted.

"It is the one with silver beads, in her box on your chest of drawers. We won't harm it. We will just put it on the winnowing basket along with the other things to be offered. The spirit making the request will just take the spirit of the necklace, and then we will return the necklace to you."

This request confused us on a number of levels. Had someone been in our bedroom and seen the necklace? Had this person relayed this information to the medium through whom the spirit allegedly spoke? Indeed, did people actually come under the influence of spirits so that spirits spoke, or was this all an illusion? Only gradually, through time, did we begin to understand the grim reality of the interaction between the Batad people and the spirit world.

What should we do? On the one hand, we wanted desperately to be receptive to the needs of our neighbors, and certainly this was a real need. A child's life was involved. On the other hand, however, we had a suspicion that there was more to this than a simple request. We simply could not just refuse to give them the necklace without some compelling reason. We had no time to think about it, no time to mull it over, no time to engage in more than a fleeting prayer.

In a flash, the answer came to me.

"We would like to help you out in whatever way we can, but this is something we cannot do." I explained that we follow the God of heaven. "He is supreme over all other beings, both in our world and the unseen world. Everything we have and own, including ourselves, belongs to him. It would be wrong now for us to take one of our possessions and let its spirit be given to another spiritual being."

They seemed to understand, perhaps even better than we. They had a perfectly good reason to explain to the spirit they were placating why they could not offer it the necklace. It had already been given to God. As they left, I encouraged them to bring their sick child to us, and we would certainly pray for it and give it medicine. This child, whom we cared for later, did recover. Incredibly, so did every child brought to us during the many years we were establishing a solid relationship with our Batad friends.

BABOT'S DEATH

It was extremely painful for us to witness our neighbors struggling with the unseen world, especially during times of sickness and death. Anita, the teenager working in our home, told us about events that surrounded the sickness of a little three-year-old girl named Babot. She was the daughter of Innawan and related to Anita. She was seriously ill. We had not yet been able to demonstrate our ability to treat sickness, so the parents did not bring Babot to us. She had a burning fever, and we suspected that she might have pneumonia. The family was poor; nevertheless, they felt that they had no choice but to call a few of the old men together to try to determine the cause of Babot's sickness and to offer a sacrifice to the spirits who had caused it. It was impossible to call spirits without something substantial to offer them, so the family provided two chickens from their little flock.

The priests murmured their prayers, killed the two chickens, and pleaded with "informer" spirits to tell them the source of Babot's sickness. One of the priests became possessed, and the other priests began talking to the spirit through their companion, who now became the medium through which the spirit talked.

The "informer" spirit gave them the name of the spirit—actually a vicious demon, which it said had caused the sickness—and immediately left. It required two more chickens to call the demon the "informer" spirit had mentioned. When the demon arrived, it immediately possessed the body of one of the priests and launched into an acrimonious demand for far more than this poor family had. Finally, it begrudgingly agreed to the remaining chickens in the family's flock.

There were more prayers and more spirits placated, and eventually all of the chickens were gone. However, instead of recovering, Babot's sickness became worse.

Anita related to us the plight of this poor family, and we urged her to try to persuade the family to come to us for medical help. But the family was unwilling to do this. What if the demon or demons causing the sickness became offended and killed Babot? So the priests continued their prayers and pleading. This was now the third day of sacrificing with no success. The family did have an ancient Ming jar that had been passed down to them from centuries past. They sold the jar and now had money to purchase a couple of pigs. The pigs were sacrificed. Surely this sacrifice would appease the anger of the demons, and they would allow Babot to recover, but it didn't happen. There were more demands made, and finally, the very last of their possessions, a rice field, was sold.

Prayers and sacrificing continued throughout the week until finally nothing was left. Babot died. The family and friends were crushed. In the shimmering heat of an early afternoon sun, a band of mourners took the lifeless body of little Babot across rice terraces, along a path, and to the mountain on the other side. There they buried her in a shallow grave.

Shadows crept slowly down the mountainsides, and a moonless night covered the landscape with the myriad of twinkling stars that filled the heavens. A gathering of Babot's parents' close relatives sat quietly under a house, reliving the events of the past days. Eventually they noticed that Babot's grandfather was not among them. Where could he be? He was nowhere to be found.

Then someone noticed a small flickering light that pierced the darkness on the other side of the valley beside the grave of Babot. Among the Ifugao people, as in many other places in the Philippines, it is common belief that flickering lights indicate the presence of a recently deceased person; that might explain the light. On the other hand, it might indicate that Babot's grandfather was at the grave site.

Two of the braver men agreed to go over to investigate. There they found Babot's grandfather. He was sitting beside the grave with a little light, a bottle filled with kerosene with a wick. Beside him lay a bolo with which he intended to end his life.

"Life is not worth living," he wailed. "We have given everything to the demons for the life of my precious granddaughter, and still, in their cruelty, they have taken her from us. What is there to live for? I want to die."

In the end, they persuaded him to go back home and go on living despite the seeming hopelessness of it all.

OUR HOME, A REFUGE
BAHHIN EXPLAINS OUR SIESTAS

Our home became a place where people could come for help with physical problems and relief from torment inflicted by the unseen spirit world. We had no idea why our neighbors considered us experts in dealing with sickness and accidents.

We had been in our Batad home about a week when four strong men brought to us a fifth man, whom they carried on a stretcher. A sixth man holding a shaft of some sort walked alongside the stretcher. As they laid the unfortunate victim on the floor of our porch, I realized that the shaft was a portion of a spear protruding from the calf of the hapless man's leg. The spearhead, including two ugly barbs, was firmly embedded in the calf. Just the point protruded from the other side. The barbs, as they were designed to do, effectively prevented the spear from being withdrawn.

Why had they brought this man here? What could they possibly expect me to do? I was a linguist, a translator. I worked at a desk with language, not surgery. I had absolutely no experience with such matters. I realized that they had not the faintest notion of why we were here, what we were here to do, or what our abilities were. Nor did they seem to care. I was from the outside, and they knew that in the outside world, we dealt with such matters and far worse. They had heard stories of men who could cut people open, extract and replace defective parts, and close them up again. I was one of them, wasn't I?

So, on that fateful night, we waded into our first case of surgery in Batad. And with it we lost any hope of avoiding the practice of medicine, no matter how ill equipped we were.

As I stood assessing the situation, I realized that the spear could not be retracted. It would have to pass through the calf. I knew that to drag the whole shaft through such a wound was bound to be extremely painful, would create an even larger wound, and could introduce massive infection. Our only option was to get a saw and cut off the shaft, even though it was an expensive heirloom. The head would now have to be pushed through, but how could we possibly do that without some sort of anesthesia? We had none. We were completely unprepared for situations such as this. We tried our best to explain what must be done.

After much discussion, most of which we could not understand, all of them, including the patient, indicated that we should proceed. We disinfected the sawn-off shaft end as best we could, put it to the remaining shaft stub and spear head, and pushed. The pain was, of course, excruciating. Experiencing this gruesome episode was almost more than I could tolerate. However, the patient survived without fainting, and I barely did also. We cleaned the two gaping wounds—one where the spear entered and the other where it exited—closed them with butterfly bandages, and applied topical medicine. We bandaged up the leg and hoped for the best.

For the next week this man and his friends were constantly in our house chattering incessantly. In this way, we got our first major exposure to their language. In a week, he was able to walk and go home. Our first medical experience was singularly successful; our reputation as healers spread far and wide, and our medical work among the Batad Ifugao was launched.

As our neighbors became more and more acquainted with us and began to understand our relationship with the unseen world, they gradually understood that the world of evil spirits held no power over us. Every small parcel of land in Batad is reported to have a resident spirit, commonly called a place spirit. This is not only true of places where people live, but also of vacant areas within the village. So when we chose a hillside and terraced it for a house, there was, they said, a spirit already living there. They declared that at times when we were in Batad, that spirit would leave our property, but when we were away, it would return and take up residence under our porch. This was affirmed by men who claimed to have the ability to see spirits.

There was no way, of course, for us to verify or refute their claims. In any event, we were not there to change their worldviews regarding the supernatural world, so we made no attempt to do so. If any aspects of their worldview were to be changed, we determined that it would be done not by us but by the Holy Spirit using God's word.

As a result of our neighbors' belief that we were not subject to demonic powers, our house often became a refuge for those who felt that they were under demonic attack. One evening, while we were relaxing after a day's work on the Ifugao language, there was a knock at our door. There stood a very worried Ilat, his wife, Inyap, and their three children. Two little ones clung to Inyap's skirt, and Ilat carried Alice, their two-year-old, wrapped in a blanket. Alice was crying incessantly. She was extremely agitated, throwing her head from side to side. Her tiny hands were picking at her clothing.

"She's being tormented by an evil spirit," Ilat informed us. "We would like to spend the night here in your house."

We invited the family inside, and we prayed fervently that God would protect this precious little life, her family, and all of us. I took the little body of Alice from Ilat, removed the blanket, and realized that she was burning with fever. After giving her medicine and doing what we could to relieve the fever, the agitation that Alice was experiencing subsided, and she fell asleep. The little family spread out their blankets on our living room floor and prepared for bed. We were thankful that we could, in this small way, provide some help to our Ifugao friends.

Once in the early years before anyone in Batad confessed Christ as their Lord and Savior, when it was necessary for us to be seven hundred miles away at Nasuli on the Island of Mindanao, we received an urgent call from our Batad neighbors. By this time, many of them understood the function of our two-way radio and that it was possible to talk to us in this way. We had disconnected our own short-wave radio, but our neighbors were aware that there was one in Banaue, our market town, operated by Doctor Irvine, a missionary medical doctor who had set up a medical clinic there. By way of the shortwave radio, he was provided medical advice to several outlying stations, like us, who were involved in giving medical help to those with whom they worked. Word came to us.

"Your friends in Batad are at the radio station in Banaue and want to speak with you."

We listened as they told us of an extremely sad situation. During the week that we had been away, five people had died violently. They went on to explain how each had died. Two had fallen from banks in their rice fields, one had died when a huge stone rolled down from an upland field, and two others had died accidentally at home. This they attributed to the fury of demons that, because of our absence, had been able to unleash their rage on the village.

We could hardly believe what they were telling us. We hastened back to Batad and heard the full story of what they firmly believed. They told us that during times when we were living with them in the village, the power of spirits over them was noticeably decreased, but when we were away, demons seemed to be free to do their damnable deeds. If this was true—and we had no way of knowing whether it was—then while we lived in Batad, the presence of the Holy Spirit was not only the source of our protection but was a protection for our Batad friends as well.

3

THE EARLY YEARS

EVERYONE HAS A TALENT

Bubbud, Bon'og, and a few others were building an addition to the stone retaining wall on our little patch of property. It never ceased to amaze me how they could do this without the use of mortar to hold the stones rigidly together.

Somewhat foolishly, I suppose, I had actually tried to build a small stone retaining wall by myself. I wasn't a complete novice, since I had often watched the men build walls. On a couple of occasions, they had shown me how to sort rocks, look critically at the spaces, find the right rocks, and fit them in. I thought my little wall looked quite acceptable, but, under heavy rains, within a week it collapsed. Many Ifugao walls had lasted for centuries. I realized that there was more to stone wall building than met the eye of a novice.

When they placed their rocks, it was possible to walk along the top edge, at any stage of construction, without a hint of rock movement. Without the aid of geometric instruments or any other mechanical device, the wall was built to slope inward at the exact angle necessary to prevent it from falling outward yet maximize the precious space of level ground behind it. When a wall was finished, it was always dead level. Not only was the terrace wall structurally sound but the builders were creating an exquisitely artistic pattern. Looking at the rock face, I could discern a graceful configuration of swirling rock, beginning with huge boulders at the base and gradually decreasing in size to small rocks at the wall cap.

As work on the wall addition progressed, I sat on my haunches Ifugao-style, watching Bubbud and the others with intense interest. Certainly they were masters of their craft, but I thought that I might be able to add something to the process. Accordingly, I made a suggestion.

"How about using this selection of rocks in the section of the wall higher up, there on the right?" This seemed reasonable to me, and I wanted them to know that I was taking an active interest in their work.

A few months earlier, when Bubbud had first begun working with me at the desk, he was timid, and I found it difficult to persuade him to be forthright in making suggestions and correcting my Ifugao, which was still quite imperfect. However, over the months, as his reserve gradually diminished, he was gaining confidence and becoming bolder. Today, building a stone wall, he was on familiar ground. This was his expertise. He brought himself up to his full five feet, four inches with a smile on his face.

"Bullay," he said in Ifugao with a clear convincing voice, "you know all about working at a desk. You are an expert in making books. That is your gift. We have gifts, too, and one is to make stone walls. We respect the decisions you make at the desk, and we know that you respect our decisions in stone masonry."

He resumed his work, and I knew that he was right. He did respect my decisions at the desk, though at this stage he could not begin to guess what transforming effects it would have on their lives. I knew, too, and respected the fact that they were experts in their field of work. That day I decided that I would be content to be an interested observer of a complex and artful activity. I was reminded of the saying, "There are different kinds of service, but the same Lord.... The body is a unit, though it is made up of many parts" (1 Corinthians 12:5, 12a).

FINDING A PATH THROUGH THE TERRACE MAZE

Ifugao rice terraces are striking indeed—striking to view, that is. I never tired of looking out on the far side of the mountain to admire the lush, green fields, especially after the walls had been weeded and repaired. Ever changing in hue, they ranged from yellow green in full sunlight to aquamarine in deep shade after transplanting of seedlings had been completed. With the approach of the harvest season, they ranged from light yellow ochre, to raw sienna, and to almost dark violet in deep shade. After heavy rains, innumerable little waterfalls fell from terrace to terrace, and the roar of water cascading through runoff canals was thunderous.

As I sat on our porch, I often traced the intricacies of the terraces as they faithfully followed the twists and turns of the landscape. One wall would begin, extend for some distance, and then come to an end at a terrace wall. A terrace above and one below would continue. This pattern was repeated over and over, but eventually all walls ended at one of two drainage canals that ran down the mountainside.

I had little difficulty navigating these narrow paths so long as I was accompanied by fellow villagers. Ifugao people have a keen sense of humor, and on one occasion as I walked with a few men along the terrace walls, one man shouted out for everyone to hear.

"Bullay is drunk! Bullay is drunk!"

What could I do or say? I may have been walking a bit unsteadily as I tried to keep up with these men who found walking on the uneven paths no more difficult than I would on a sidewalk back home. I could only hope that my reputation by this time was well enough established for amused watchers to realize that this was just a mischievous joke.

My confidence increased greatly, however, when on one occasion I was accompanying a group of visiting American soldiers along those dikes, and some were so unsteady on their feet that they resorted to crawling on all fours. Falling allowed two choices: one could either fall into the terrace of the dike on which they walked and sink into six inches of soft, gooey mud—destroying the growing rice in the process—or fall down the embankment into the field below, with possibly more severe consequences. For the uninitiated terrace walker, the tendency was to lean into the terrace on which one walked. We often had to apologize to the local people for the substantial destruction caused when our visitors ended up in the rice fields.

During my childhood I attended a summer camp that was located near a railway track. The other children and I spent hours walking on the rails to see who would be first to fall off. With practice over the years, I could walk for miles on those thin rails without once having to put a foot on the ground beside it for balance. This childhood game undoubtedly saved me from many falls on the Batad terrace walls.

From the vantage point of our veranda it was impossible to trace the little path that ran along the dike edges from the hamlet of Higib on the left through the expanse of terraces to Bo'oh on the right. There were times when I was out on those terraces alone, and these times were often quite embarrassing. The problem was that not only could we watch what went on in those fields from our veranda, but so could our neighbors who lived in the various hamlets that dotted the Batad Valley.

Finding my way anywhere was not one of my strong suits. Neighbors would watch with great amusement as I set out, trying to keep track of the proper dikes on which to walk. I could usually do this since they were, in general, more worn and had fewer weeds than other dikes. Terraces that had been newly prepared for transplanting, however, all looked the same to me. I would often fail to climb to a terrace above or below, continuing on to the end of that terrace wall. At the end I might have found little jutting stones in the wall that would allow me to climb up or down to another dike, and if so, I would keep going. Eventually, though, I would reach a point where I would have to go up or down, and there might be no jutting steps in the wall. Some walls were up to ten feet high, and in that case there was nothing to do but retrace my steps. Sometimes I would simply scale the bank and continue on. My activities provided great amusement for onlookers. I would always either make it across by myself by sheer effort and determination or be rescued by a sympathetic passerby and directed back to the right path.

THE BATAD "AIRSTRIP"

We entertained no hope of ever reaching Batad in any way other than hiking in over the formidable mountain that separated us from the outside world. The idea of air transportation was not even considered. It was ludicrous. This land stood on end. Not a single sizeable patch of level ground existed that had not been laboriously leveled by skilled laborers. Maybe a helicopter could land near Batad, but we had no such expensive vehicle. We did have a small airplane that could land on short runways, but it was not in Batad. Not with all the skill of our willing and helpful neighbors could we imagine a strip long enough and wide enough for a landing.

Our neighbors, though, had other ideas. They knew nothing about airplanes, but they knew they could turn a rugged mountain ridge into level ground. There was such a place that could be leveled, they assured us. It was high in one of the nearby mountains. They wanted to take us there for a look.

The first kilometer or so of our trek was relatively easy. It snaked along a little trail that climbed ever higher. Then we left the luxury of the path and began to climb in earnest through a dense forest. I was in good physical shape. I had hiked over the mountain into our Batad home countless times and, when necessary, was able to reach the summit at a brisk pace without resting.

This, though, was not a path. It was a mountain face, and it seemed to me that it went straight up. However, if Ifugao men could scale it without great effort and without resting, then I should be able to do it, too. I wanted to prove that I, too, was an Ifugao. But I could not. My chest heaved, and my breath came in great gasps. To be a true Ifugao, I would have had to be born one, to have lived and climbed on these steep slopes from the time that I had learned to walk.

So with halting gasps, I was forced to confess, "We'll have to stop. I can't go on without resting."

My friends, tolerant, as always, of the weaknesses of outsiders, found little ledges where they squatted on their haunches, exchanged pepper leaves or nuts, and chewed betel nut. After several rests of this kind, we finally reached the ridge. Try as I might, I could not see anything that faintly looked like the potential for an airstrip.

We paced, we measured, and we even slashed and dug, but in the end, it was hopeless. To clear a strip of land long enough and level enough for even an airplane capable of short takeoffs and landings, there must be something to work with. This land just didn't lend itself to the possibility. So we gave up and contented ourselves with hiking over the Batad Mountain for the length of our Ifugao stay.

DOREEN'S DILEMMA IN WET TERRACE FARMING

Our neighbors knew that we would never be rich by Ifugao standards. Yet, since we were the children of Mannong, one of the richest men in Batad, something had to be done. Riches were measured by the number of rice fields held and by the number and age of rice wine jars. Some jars were glazed brown and undecorated, others were coarse buff stoneware dragon jars, and still others were blue and white or red and blue on white Ming jars with elaborate floral designs. Both plain and ornate jars had been traded with China as early as the fourteenth century during the Ming Dynasty. Trading continued into the Ching Dynasty of the seventeenth and eighteenth centuries.

However, all trace of commerce with China was lost to the Ifugao people, and in its place had developed folk legends of the supernatural origins of precious possessions. Mannong could not just give us one of those jars. That would be far too risky, since he knew that the day would probably come when we would leave Batad with our children, along with a valuable inheritance such as a wine jar. A rice field seemed far more practical, since it would obviously remain in Batad. So Doreen became the owner of one of Mannong's terraced fields.

Doreen's rice field was a little terrace among the massive sweep of Batad rice terraces. She maintained this terrace until we left Batad in 1971.

We were delighted with this gift. We now actually had a little strip of land on that magnificent mountainside. We were part of Ifugao history. We conjectured that that terrace had likely been there for at least several hundreds of years.

Friendly neighbors and relatives eagerly began to teach Doreen the intricacies of terrace agriculture. They taught her to cling to the wall by using her toes like gripping fingers, thereby freeing her hands to pull weeds. They showed her how to stomp those weeds into the soft mud as soil-enriching fertilizer. They taught her the intricacies of the irrigation system, the need to keep water channels clear of weeds and debris. They taught her how to maintain mudfish, snails, and shells within her terrace as food, along with the rice that would eventually be planted in her plot. They taught her how to build and plant seedbeds and how to take the resulting seedlings and transplant them into the soft mud. They also taught her water level control within her field.

However, Doreen failed to faithfully follow this last important lesson. She did not maintain a constant flow of water into her terraced field. She understood the basic rules of water rights—who could get water first when there wasn't enough for everyone—and that it was necessary to safeguard those rights by constantly inspecting the canals to be sure the water was flowing where it should and was not being diverted into someone else's field. However, to safeguard those rights, it would have been necessary for Doreen to sleep in the fields beside her terrace along with many other people guarding theirs. She wanted to be an Ifugao, to take her place in the agricultural system of rice growing, but she was unwilling to pay this price. Each day she would find her water flowing into someone else's field. She would restore the flow only to find it diverted again the next day. So, little by little, the water level in her field diminished, until finally the field dried up. She could only hope for a more abundant water supply the next year.

FROGS, TERMITES, AND OTHER DANGERS

Our children were better at being Ifugaos than we were. Children learn by observing and imitating, and our children were as good as any good little Ifugao at that. They learned the Ifugao language quickly; they learned to eat and relish Ifugao food; and they learned to conduct themselves as Ifugao children.

Gordon had just celebrated his second birthday when Doreen noticed him acting in a rather suspicious manner. She tried to see what he was concealing in his hand, but he ran and quickly hopped into his crib, pulled his blankets over him, and announced, "*Mi'id itlug! Mi'id itlug!*" (I don't have an egg! I don't have an egg!)

On another occasion, Gordon came home from playing with a neighbor's son, and protruding from his mouth was the leg of a frog. Doreen almost fainted, but she needn't have. It was undoubtedly appropriately boiled and completely palatable, an Ifugao delicacy.

Sometimes when termites migrate to new locations to establish new colonies, they grow wings and fly in huge swarms. Our children, as enthusiastically as any other Ifugao child, would catch these termites, pull off their wings, and eat them. They insisted that they tasted as delicious as any candy eaten by children in the outside world, and we had to admit that they were probably much healthier for them. We never did get accustomed to watching our children engage in this pleasurable pastime, however.

Visitors from the world outside our valley were always surprised—perhaps shocked—that we didn't have a fence around our house yard. We were situated on a little ledge, with a reclining bank below us that kept on sloping downward until it reached the river several hundred meters below. How could children play in a yard such as that without the protection of a fence? However, our children, as well as all Ifugao children, are keenly aware of heights. It is built into Ifugao children from birth, and they are as sure-footed as mountain goats. Our children imitated them with equal agility. Not once did they fall from our yard or from any of the countless other dangerous places which might be disastrous for other children. We often saw them running and skipping along narrow terrace dikes. They, far more than Doreen and I, were true Ifugaos.

Bahhin was our mother. She and Mannong, our father, were our go-betweens to negotiate any matter of concern between us and our neighbors. Bahhin took it upon herself to explain our peculiarities to those around us who viewed us with much curiosity.

During our time in Manila, we had adopted the pleasant practice of taking a short siesta in the middle of the day. Although sleeping at this time in Ifugao was unheard of, except for someone either lazy or sick, we had maintained this practice. Of course, being a night owl, I was accustomed to working into the night, sometimes as late as midnight. This habit was also very different from usual Ifugao behavior. Our neighbors, coming home from some late-night event, would inevitably see our windows illuminated by our kerosene pressure lamp.

We had explained to Bahhin and our other Ifugao friends that when it was daytime in our country, it was nighttime in Ifugao, and vice versa. This provided Bahhin with a completely plausible explanation for those curious about our unusual behavior.

"You see," she explained, with an air of knowledge, "noontime is midnight in their country, so of course they want to sleep at noon. When night comes here, it is daylight there, so they want to work during their daytime."

We let the explanation stand.

OUR FIRST IFUGAO CHRISTMAS

It was January when we first arrived in Batad, so we had a whole year to learn the Batad Ifugao language before Christmas came around. During this time we had explained that God had sent his son Jesus to earth, that he had been born of a virgin, had lived until young manhood, and then had been killed by wicked men who nailed him to a cross erected on a hill along with two thieves. All of this, we explained, was in punishment for our sins, so that we could live with him forever.

No matter how much we tried, we could not convince anyone to trust Jesus Christ for help in this life and salvation in the next. Invariably, we were told, "That's very good for you because you are different. You are not true Ifugaos. You see, each one of us has been given over to the spirits of the unseen world. We belong to them. We must obey them and offer sacrifices to them. To do otherwise would be to bring calamity to our lives and the lives of our children. Our crops would not produce fruit. We would become sick and die. In addition, it would expose us to great catastrophe and calamity in the next life. You are very fortunate that you worship a loving god. Our gods are cruel, and we would not dare anger them by worshipping any other god."

Some Ifugao neighbors had learned to trust us for many of their medical needs, but with their very lives? This was too much to ask.

In the process of discussing the coming of Jesus to earth, we explained that December 25 was the day each year when we remember his birth. Jesus was God's precious gift to all of us. So, to remember and celebrate that, we make Christmas Day a special day, and we exchange gifts with each other.

Days before December 25, people began to tell us that they would come to our house for their *Kulihmat*. What that meant we had no idea, but we assumed it had something to do with celebrating Christmas with us. The day arrived, and people started coming. Each one bore a gift—an egg, a small can of rice, a mudfish, a bundle of taro leaves or root, fermented rice grains (considered a delicacy), and bananas. Yet after delivering their gifts, they did not go home.

"We will wait for our *Kulihmat*," they informed us.

Were they waiting for a gift from us? As the day progressed, more and more people came until there were hundreds milling around our house and yard.

Finally, Lab'an, our household helper, explained what our neighbors were waiting for. They expected us to put on a program of some sort for them. We were flabbergasted. We were not performers. We didn't sing or dance in public. What could we offer them?

In the end, we sat down and planned a program that would be our attempt at celebrating our first Christmas with these beautiful people. We had a ukulele to accompany us in singing carols in English and a couple of Ifugao songs we had translated, including "The Love of God." We could read our first attempt at translating the Christmas story from Mathew's Gospel. A couple of ladies, including one from England, were with us, and they could dance a couple of English folk dances. So our program began to take shape.

In spite of our croaking and stumbling in Ifugao and our completely unprofessional performance, in the end, what we offered was apparently a great success. Gallons and gallons of fruit juice made from our cans of powdered juice mix were distributed so each guest could get at least a taste of our *bayah*, or "rice wine." Our friends and neighbors went home that evening satisfied with the knowledge that they had given us our *Kulihmat* and that, in return, we had favored them with their *Kulihmat*. Our prayer that night was that they would, by the events of this day, begin to realize that the greatest *Kulihmat* that they could receive was God's precious gift to them.

CARRYING "SARDINES" TO BATAD

Our grocery stock was running low. I had made a quick trip to the nearest place outside of Ifugao to get some supplies—typing paper, carbon paper, pencils, pens, and a few groceries. Included on the shopping list was a case of sardines. I arrived in Dalican late in the afternoon. The first breath of night wind stirred through the Dalican valley, slanting smoke from small upland fires into the mountains to meet the descending shadows of oncoming night. I was in a hurry to get home, but I could not come empty-handed. We had not tasted meat for several days, so perhaps I could manage the case of sardines. It was heavy—about eighty pounds—but I could rig up a harness to carry it on my back. But that mountain!

By the time I parked my jeep and hiked the one kilometer down the road to the little trail that veered off to the left and upward to the summit, the mountain was already in shadow and sharply violet against the darkening sky. I probably should have left the sardines behind and carried something lighter. However, the anticipation of eating meat again was strong, and I began the steep ascent with the box on my back. It was torturous. I was forced to rest several times along the way, but through brute determination I finally made the summit. Too exhausted to realize what I was doing I released the burden from my back too near the edge of a steep incline. No sooner had I put it down than it went tumbling down the steep bank landing several meters below, caught in some tangled bushes. I was tempted to leave it behind, but again the anticipation of a delicious meal overcame me, and I scrambled down the bank and retrieved the box and carried it back up.

By the time I reached home, the sky had darkened from dusty green to midnight blue, and all I could see were black, shapeless forms of trees and shrubs. Doreen lovingly greeted me, and we eagerly opened the box for a can of sardines and a delicious supper. To our utter amazement and my frustration, there wasn't a can of sardines in the box—it was filled with cans of squid! I could have sat there and cried, but that would have done no good. So we both had a hearty laugh as I told her the story of the runaway box of squid.

ON WINGS OF ANGELS

It was a late Saturday evening. Again I had been out for supplies, this time to Manila. All day Friday I had been busy buying supplies for the next three months that Doreen and I would be shut away in the mountain fastness of Batad—away from friends and colleagues, away from access to the physical needs that our lives had taught us were so necessary for normal living. Anxious to get home to my wife and work, I left Manila at about six in the morning. Twelve hours later, I arrived at our garage clinging to the mountainside in Dalican, and parked our Jeep.

I had made that trip from Manila, up the eastern side of the island of Luzon, through several provinces, and finally into Ifugao Province many times but rarely in one day. Doreen and I usually traveled together and were met in Dalican in midafternoons by our Batad neighbors, who patiently waited to carry our supplies over the mountain into Batad.

Usually, with Doreen following me up the trail to keep me company and with others in front and behind, the steep twelve-hundred-foot climb to the pass and then the descent on the other side didn't seem too difficult. God's glorious nature provided endless beauty and surprises. There were myriad tropical and subtropical plants and flowers along the way.

In wetter areas—where little mountain streams tumbled over craggy rocks shaded by a profusion of higher, leafy growth—delicate blue violet-like flowers clung tentatively to the dampened moss. Ferns in abundance decorated the mountain landscape. There was the delicate lacy-leafed maidenhair and countless other varieties. Occasionally the stately tree fern would show itself. There was the exotic flamingo bush, bearing bright red flowers, and other foliage, such as the striking zebras with white veining on dark green leaves, or the ever-present mother-in-law's tongue. I often wondered who the miserable man was who named this plant, with its long, thin, tough leaves thrusting upward from the root.

We wanted to bring specimens of all this vegetation home and plant them, but, try as we would, only a few survived. Our veranda, decorated with hurricane vines—their big, leathery, deeply serrated leaves—was one of the few successful exceptions.

Occasionally we would be surprised by a small, bright red, yellow, and black ringed snake darting from our path into the thick foliage. Sometimes we saw pythons large enough to swallow rats and other forest creatures. The meter-long forest lizards were sometimes in our path, but when we came upon them, they would scurry into the anonymity of the deep forest.

On this moonless night, however, I was alone with my backpack and flashlight, with a hike of at least two hours ahead of me. By the time I had hiked the one kilometer to the head of the trail that took off at a steep angle up the mountainside, it was dark. There were no street lights here—not even the small flickering kerosene lights seeping from the windows and doorways of local residents some distance away. The only lights were the pinprick stars struggling to show themselves through puffs of dark clouds. In addition, I was tired and carried a fifty-pound load. This time I didn't have the beauty of the forest or the surprises along the way to distract me from my misery. I was only conscious of that steep and treacherous trail and the load that weighed me down.

I began contemplating the wisdom of decisions that had brought me to this place, especially at this ungodly hour. Surely there was an easier way to serve God. Had he really brought me here, or had I just made foolish choices on my own along the way?

My thoughts turned to the symbolism that I was enacting on that trail: a lost sinner with his heavy load trudging blindly into the blackness of the night with no idea of his destination or how to extricate himself from his burden. Surely this represented Ifugao men and women who were, as we were well aware, heavily burdened with cares that we knew little about—heading, along with their sins, straight for destruction.

No, it wasn't a foolish choice for me and my wife to work in this difficult place, with our children off at school a thousand kilometers away. It was not unreasonable to want to get home as quickly as possible to my loving wife.

So I labored upward. *Lord help me! Bear me up! Let this load seem not so heavy.* In my imagination it seemed that angels surrounded me. I was not alone. Suddenly the load was gone, and I sprinted forward. I was barely aware of my surroundings. In a moment, it seemed, I was at the crest of the mountain pass. Was it my imagination? I could not tell. Yet I knew one thing. One way or another, I had been borne on the wings of angels, and all that was left of this journey was a downhill jaunt to the warmth of my wife and the comforts of home.

WATCHING A TYPHOON GO BY

The island of Luzon is directly in the path of fearful typhoons that sweep across the southeastern Pacific Islands and onto the Asian mainland. Northern Luzon, where we lived, is especially hard hit and sustains extensive damage each year. Over time, however, the Ifugao people have devised ingenious housing patterns to help lessen the impact of nature's yearly rampages. Houses are built to sway like palm trees in these raging gales. I had little knowledge of how this was accomplished, although I had observed that not one nail was used in house construction. Square holes for pegs were chiseled through pairs of beams or pairs of beams and other boards where they crossed each other. Wooden pegs were pounded through these pairs to hold them securely together. In some cases, these pegs protruded below the boards they secured. Smaller cross pegs were firmly inserted through holes in the protruding peg to form an inverted T. This method of construction prevented the pegs from working loose in a storm.

Our house was tucked into the shelter of a mountain crease and escaped the full force of gales that passed through. We could stand on our porch and watch as fierce winds whipped huge sheets of rain horizontally through our valley. Ifugao houses creaked and groaned and swayed in the onslaughts, but never did we see a house succumb to these terrible storms.

The day after such storms was always an exhilarating experience. Typically, the day would be quiet and dark, full of the roar of water rushing pell-mell down the terrace-runoff canals. Terrace rockslides almost always scarred the otherwise well-groomed walls that had not been able to withstand the lashing torrents. This spelled hours or days of backbreaking work for the men to restore them to their magnificent beauty. Eventually the clouds that covered the valley would lift, and glorious sunshine, which sometimes we had not seen for a week or more, would break through. This, like Noah's rainbow, would be our promise that the radiance of God's Gospel would eventually break through the darkness of hearts that from time immemorial had known nothing of the enlightening brilliance of that Message.

MAGIC AND MORALITY

One of the amazing things that we discovered in our intimate association with our Batad village friends was their honesty. Our neighbors, for the most part, lived outside the control of a national government with its rules and laws. They had little or no contact with major religions. We assumed that people who were headhunters and demon worshipers would have little moral or social control.

The more we became intimately acquainted with our Ifugao neighbors, however, the more we realized that we needed to alter our view of their values. Gradually we came to realize that in the areas of morality and social interaction, they were generally more regulated and controlled by their intricate system than were people who had adopted Christianity or other major forms of religion. They were surely more moral and controlled than many people back home. Committing adultery, for example, was a major crime in Ifugao. It involved a man (either married or single) and a married woman. If the woman was single, neither the man nor the woman was considered to have committed adultery. A male adulterer or his family would be subjected to severe fines involving the payment of numerous items, such as cooking vats, bolos, spears, digging bars, blankets, and pigs. He would pay these fines not only to the husband and close relatives of the adulterous woman but also to her children and close relatives, as well as to his wife and her close relatives. Failing this, the adulterer would be killed. Only on rare occasions would an adulterous woman be fined. For this, she would need to be proven the aggressor in the relationship. She would pay substantial fines to her husband and his close relatives and to her adulterous partner's wife and her close relatives.

The traditional Ifugao concept of morality, however, is different from what we understand from the scriptures. Unmarried children beyond the age of four or five through the teenage years, until marriage, slept in single boys' or single girls' sleeping houses. Married men often visited the girls' sleeping houses to socialize and have intimate relations with them. In discussing this with one of my language helpers who was married with several children, I asked him if he ever visited the girls' sleeping houses.

"Yes, sometimes I do, if my wife is kind to me," he answered. Obviously, the traditional Ifugao system of laws, rules, and regulations differs from what is taught in the Bible.

Theft, when we arrived in Batad, was virtually unknown. On one occasion, we made a trip outside Ifugao. Upon our return, some three weeks later, we discovered that we had forgotten to close one bedroom window. We expected that our belongings would have been pilfered, but it turned out that no one had entered our house. Everything was exactly as we had left it.

On another occasion, when we were away, the person we left in charge of watching our house noticed that a spray gun with insecticide—which we kept in our outdoor toilet to control flies and odor—was missing. That night he resorted to the Ifugao practice of announcing something for the whole village to hear.

He stood at the edge of our yard and shouted, "Whoever took our spray gun had better return it. If they do not, there will be an investigation!"

The next morning, the spray gun was back in its place. Theft, of course, was not unknown. When it did occur, it usually involved expensive items that could be concealed, such as arm bracelets or other expensive jewelry. Magic, involving the unseen world, was used to control violations of moral laws.

Our neighbors had observed that we outsiders also dealt in magic. Our magic involved machines of some sort. They had seen us capture their voices and conversations in a box, which we called a tape recorder, to which was attached nothing more than a cord with a metal ball and handle at the end. By pushing a button, the voices would come back out. An amazing thing was that even though the voices came out, somehow they were still inside, since they would come out again and again with the push of the button. Another box somehow allowed these foreigners to talk to someone who seemed to be inside the box. Whom they talked to and how they could be small enough to be inside the box was a major miracle. Surely, from the Ifugaos' point of view, these outsiders dealt with miraculous things.

Ifugaos could catch thieves by appealing to the unseen world. There was a class of informer spirits who, if they were offered enough pigs and chickens, would inform on the guilty party when a theft had occurred. One of the more common indicators of theft involved the "hot water treatment." A cauldron of water would be placed over a roaring fire. Fine ashes would be added to the water to increase the temperature of the resulting gruel when it boiled. Then all suspects of a theft would line up and, one by one, thrust a hand into the boiling cauldron. Those who were innocent of the offence would not be burned. Those who were guilty would be severely burned, or so we were told. Whenever we watched, the guilty person would refuse to plunge a hand into the liquid, thus revealing his or her guilt. This method required the sacrifice of expensive pigs and several chickens so, unless the item stolen was excessively expensive, it was not worth the price of a costly sacrifice.

One woman, attempting to avoid the high cost of the "hot water treatment," had an ingenious idea: why not appeal to the magic of the foreigners? So she came to our house with a puzzling question.

"Do you have a machine that can catch a thief?" she inquired.

Without knowledge of the background surrounding this question, I had no idea what she might be asking. However, as we talked, I gradually understood her question. If we could record voices, and if we could talk to people who could not be seen, then perhaps we also had a box of some sort that would somehow indicate a thief.

At first I was tempted to laugh. Surely this woman who sought the help of our "magic" had no idea about the difference between Ifugao magic and what we from the outside can do with technology. Then I realized that indeed we did have a box that could—with partial accuracy, at least—indicate when a person was telling the truth or was lying. So I explained to her what we had in our country. I also told her that these machines, polygraph machines, were expensive, and only those who were involved in enforcing our laws used them. So, unfortunately, I could not help her.

CULTURE AND DRESS

One goal during our stay with our Ifugao friends was to become as much like them in appearance and practice as we could. Doreen adopted the dress of an Ifugao woman—a wraparound multicolored skirt with a pompom belt. With her dark hair, she fit in nicely.

It was a bit more difficult for me. Men generally wore loincloths. In such a rugged, mountainous area with hues from dark green to dusty blue-gray and ordered, lush, green terraces, their muscular, bronzed bodies, largely uncovered, blended in nicely with their environment. With flowing red, yellow, and dark blue loincloth tails both in front and back, and with their scabbards and shining bolos at their sides whenever they left home, their dress appeared not only acceptable but almost stately.

However, the attire looked entirely different on a white man. The stark chalkiness of a white body was completely out of place and gave the impression of nakedness. I simply refused to be seen in public—or even in private with anyone but my wife—with nothing on except a loincloth. So I had to go with plan B—that is, to wear what a few men were beginning to wear, a white undershirt with short sleeves, a pair of shorts, and slip-on sandals.

When we were with our friends away from our house, we tried to sit as they did. They did not have chairs to sit on. Some did have yard benches that served as a place to sit and sometimes to sleep. However, I found squatting on my haunches, as they usually did, almost impossible to imitate. Gradually, however, as we became more accustomed to living in Ifugao, it seemed quite natural and restful to assume that position, sometimes for extended periods of time while conversing with friends.

Our food was also much like Ifugao cuisine. We ate rice and sweet potatoes as our staple foods almost exclusively. Sometimes they were supplemented with a little meat and some vegetables. Our close friends would have liked to see us eating typical Ifugao protein—mudfish and other aquatic life from the pond fields—and, occasionally, we were supplied with such delicacies, which we ate with relish. This food, however, was available only at the end of harvest season.

Since the fields were planted with crops twice a year, the fields were not often without growing rice. The Ifugao women always carried a little can tied around their waists at one side when they worked either in their upland or pond fields. As they worked, usually weeding, they would watch for anything crawling, and this would immediately be popped into their cans. By late afternoon, they usually had enough protein for their evening meal. They often wanted to share these morsels with us. We were able to explain to Bahhin, our Ifugao mother, that we were not accustomed to eating that kind of food. She would have an expression on her face that said, "You do not know what you are missing!" But she graciously accepted the fact that we were declining her gift. After all, she declined some of our food, too.

One day we were eating a lettuce salad, a rare treat that we had brought in from outside. She tried a bite and promptly rushed outside to spit it out. "Inedible!" she commented. For others, it was necessary to be more careful about what we declined, and on occasion, we accepted gifts of "food" that we simply could not eat.

We would have liked to live in an Ifugao-style house, but this just wasn't practical for us. We were there to work at desks, so we needed rooms with tables, chairs, and windows that would let in light so we could write and type our materials. Besides, we had to admit that we were *Melikanos*. We were far too soft for Ifugao-style living. We needed beds with thick mattresses and comfortable chairs with cushioned seats and footstools where we could relax and read during the long evening hours.

One major contrast between our ways and those of our Ifugao friends involved the general area of death. When someone died, they were not embalmed, put in a silk-lined casket, and displayed for mourners to see in a sleeping repose with flowers and candles. In Ifugao, people were tied sitting up in death chairs without being embalmed and kept in them for up to three weeks or longer, depending on the status of the dead person and the number of children left behind. A death chair consisted of a back frame against which the dead person rested, sitting on a small frame seat. The head was tied at the forehead to the back of the frame with a loincloth or woman's belt. For as long as the person remained in the chair, someone with a fly switch would sit in front and shoo away flies twenty-four hours a day.

The dead person would remain at one child's house for three or four days and then be transferred to the next. To transport a body was an unpleasant activity, to put it mildly. In order to be able to endure this job, the carrier often became somewhat drunk to numb the shock involved. The body would be placed piggy-back-style on the back of the carrier for transporting. We visited many of these sessions. Older folk sat around talking and chewing betel nut while children played and laughed, often playing tops or hopscotch nearby. There was little outward evidence of quiet reverence for the dead person.

In Batad, the dead were not buried in graves dug into the ground. They were placed in caves that were dug out of the mountainsides and had openings about three feet high and three feet wide. On one occasion, I had the opportunity to crawl into one of these caves. The dead were completely wrapped in burial blankets and tied with the head at the top and feet below in a squatting position. A few bones were scattered on the cave floor, and I assumed these were the remains of unidentified ancestors.

Regardless of these differences, however, after several years we did manage—at least to some extent—to almost become Ifugaos culturally and linguistically. One time, several of us men were squatting in a circle on our haunches discussing matters of particular interest to Ifugaos. Gahhid, a young man of the village, was in the process of going through the various marriage rituals in taking a young bride, Kalumay. We were discussing the computation of a dowry for Kalumay, who was the oldest daughter of a wealthy family. Her parents and family would receive several chickens for the engagement payment, a pig for the prenuptial payment, a very large pig for the marriage payment, and six pigs and a few chickens each for the first, second, third, and fourth post-marriage payments. Although Gahhid and Kalumay would be considered married upon receipt of the marriage payment and could live together as husband and wife, Gahhid and his family would still be obliged to pay the post-marriage bride-price payments to seal the marriage. If they failed to do this within a reasonable time, the marriage would be dissolved, and the bride's family would keep the payments already given.

The conversation gradually drifted to recent events that would almost certainly change the way people lived. Tourists in larger and larger numbers were beginning to encroach on this mountain fastness. Bon'og told us of difficulties he experienced recently when he went to Banaue to shop for salt and sugar. He wore his loincloth, carried his spear, and wore a deerskin utility backpack. This was normal dress for an Ifugao man. But it seemed that there were pesky tourists everywhere! He would be in one store and, upon coming out, would be confronted by a tourist with a camera aimed at him. He would try to dodge getting his picture taken, but they were so rude and persistent!

Someone else described what these tourists wore: silly-looking hats, big, heavy boots, and sometimes betel nut bags, which they had bought in the market and wore on their hips to try to look like Ifugaos. An Ifugao would not be caught dead wearing a betel nut bag like that. They were to be tucked into one's belt at the back or carried in the hand. But the women! Yes, the silly hats—but shorts? They looked like men! And their legs were completely exposed! What respectful woman would ever wear shorts?

We roared with laughter as Bubbud described the antics and strange and foolish clothing of these foreigners. Then suddenly it hit me: I was one of them! I was a foreigner! Yet, for the moment, I was indeed an Ifugao looking at the world through Ifugao eyes. In this respect, at least, we had arrived. We had become Ifugaos. Being one with them, at last we were in a position to begin influencing them to take God's word as theirs, in Ifugao, and apply it to their hearts.

THE ART OF ARGUMENTATION

The Ifugao people and other groups of the mountains of Northern Luzon sometimes played a game, a verbal contest of banter, to pass the time. Usually there were two practiced players and several curious and eager onlookers. Two men or women (rarely a man and a woman) would begin talking about a particular subject—any subject, weighty or trivial—that would accommodate two opposing positions. Commonly, it would begin with an offhand remark by someone, which would be challenged by someone else. This would almost inevitably begin a bantering contest that would sometimes go on for hours. To successfully engage in such encounters, contestants needed to be masters of their language and culture and able to skillfully control veiled and hidden meanings. They also needed to have an interminable imagination for multiple facets of any given subject. Novices studiously avoided such confrontations to escape unpleasant embarrassments.

Needless to say, I diligently ducked participation in this sport, although on numerous occasions I had been challenged to compete in it. One day, though, before I realized what was happening, I was drawn into a bantering contest with Mani. He was one of the wealthiest men in Batad, but in many ways he was a carefree vagrant, bent on dissipating the family wealth on anything that would provide a moment of pleasure. In more sober moments, he loved to engage in jocularity, and, although he could hardly be considered a master of his language, he was not one to avoid a bantering contest.

I had recently returned from a trip to North America, and while there I had visited the exquisite Butchart Gardens of Victoria, where I had picked up a few flower seeds. Fueled with awe and enthusiasm at seeing how an abandoned surface mine could be turned into such gorgeous and graceful gardens, I had decided to attempt a little "Butchart Garden" of my own. Across from the stone steps that ran past our house lay a waste area of coarse imperata and miscanthus grasses along with assorted prickly vines and bushes. This would be an excellent opportunity, I thought, to clear the area, have a couple of small terraces built, and make it a place of beauty. However, there was a risk involved. No self-respecting Ifugao would waste time and energy on such a trivial and useless effort. Who ever heard of a garden of flowers? Perhaps, I reasoned, if I could improve the area without divulging just what exactly I intended to plant there, when it burst forth in all its glorious splendor, it would be appreciated.

No such luck! Somehow Mani knew full well what I intended to plant in these contour-ridged gardens. I was on our porch attending to someone who needed medical help, when Mani sauntered by. He wasted no time in thoroughly chaffing me about the useless plots I was having built.

"No, no!" I protested as vehemently as I could, putting on my best attempt to look shocked and hurt. "You've got it all wrong!" With that, he had me in a bantering contest in front of a dozen spectators, and I could not back out.

I unhappily plowed forward. I portrayed myself as a poor man with no terraces to farm, no way of putting more than a few sweet potatoes on my table, being ridiculed by a rich man with so many terraces that he could sell one on a whim! All I was trying to do was to find a little spot where I might, with a little luck, be able to eke out a meager addition to our skimpy table. He knew, I knew, and the spectators knew that the situation was nothing of the sort.

The bystanders, eager for a friendly confrontation, roared with laughter, and, coming to my aid, added fuel to the fire that I had kindled. There was no denying it. He was rich, and I—with only one paltry field given to Doreen by our father and no inherited jars to my name—was, according to Ifugao reckoning, an utter pauper. In the end, though, Mani capitulated. I had won. End of argument.

MANI AND THE VETERINARY SYRINGE

Mani was a natural target for practical jokes. It seemed that he was incessantly involved in banter and levity of one kind or another, and I bore my share of his convivial clowning. This I took as a compliment, since it marked me as an insider, one of Mani's friends. I watched for ways to reciprocate his pranks, and one day a choice opportunity seemed to present itself.

Mani was suffering from a nasty boil on his leg, and he waited on our porch for his turn to be treated. Suppurations of various kinds responded dramatically to penicillin, and under the supervision of a medical doctor on our radio net with whom we had daily contact, we were able to give injections in this remote region that was inaccessible to modern medicine.

As I worked, I hatched a plan that I was sure would be a first-rate prank. When it was Mani's turn, I said as seriously as I could, "This is a nasty boil. We'll have to give you an extra-large injection." With that, I went into our kitchen and took out a veterinary syringe with a huge needle about four inches long and filled it with water.

I came outside holding the syringe with its needle pointing up, slowly expelling some of the water as I came toward Mani. He looked at that syringe in abject horror, and before I could say a word, he fainted dead away.

It was now my turn to be horrified. I had totally underestimated Mani's reaction. I had completely forgotten to consider that, for someone not accustomed to modern medicines of any kind, even a small needle would tax an Ifugao's ability to tolerate an injection—even someone as manly as Mani. I passed smelling salts under his nose, and he slowly revived. Only his pride was injured by embarrassment, the result of my foolish joke. I apologized profusely and promised never again to mix medicine with mindless frivolity.

CLIMBING THE WALL OF TAPPIA' GULLY

Beyond the Batad terraces was the massive Tappia' Gully lying in dark purple shadows of early evening. Deep at the bottom of this gully, and out of sight from where I often sat on our veranda, rushed the Batad River. On the far gully wall was a huge outcropping of limestone known as Ubban's scar. According to legend, it was inhabited by Ubban, one of over a thousand gods of the Ifugao pantheon. In the past, and completely forgotten through time, Ubban's scar had resulted from a tremendous earth slide, which had temporarily blocked the river's flow. We were reminded of this, however, as the stillness of the night was often broken by the thunderous roar of small sections of the wall still sliding into the river.

Though we did not often hike through these wilds—preferring instead to view them from the safety of our home—we did, on occasion, take a picnic lunch down Ubban's Gully and around a bend upriver, where there was a magnificent waterfall. There, the entire Batad River, pressed into a narrow channel of solid rock and then tumbled through about thirty feet of pure bedrock to plunge headlong another seventy feet to a basin below. The continual spray thrown up by this clamorous cascade allowed tropical plants to grow in profusion in the crevices of the rock face. The basin, carved out through centuries by this massive cataract, was impressive. About a city block in size, it provided a magnificent place for picnicking and swimming.

Our Batad friends told me that if I could just climb the hundred-foot wall face of Tappia' Gully, we could easily reach another village that I had never before visited. It was a challenge. Although the cliff face was partially covered by small shrubs and plants, much of it was bare rock. I watched as some of my friends effortlessly clambered up the cliff without the aid of belaying devices or ropes. I had never attempted rock climbing, but, I reasoned, if they can do it, so can I—perhaps not with as much grace, but surely I could reach the top. So I started out, with Bubbud immediately behind me. I could not help but notice the rather concerned look on his face. Apparently, he didn't have as much faith in my ability at rock climbing as I did.

The Tappia' waterfall is about one hundred feet from top to bottom. The entire Batad River tumbles over rocks the first thirty feet, then plunges straight down the final seventy feet or so. A huge basin, about a hectare in size, has been carved out by falling water at the base of the waterfall.

That wall was high! The roar of the falls was deafening as I started my ascent. At twenty feet I was still climbing, though I was having difficulty finding horizontal creases wide enough for firm footholds. My friends, barefooted, had the advantage of what amounted to four hands. With shoes, climbing was much more awkward. At thirty feet, I made the mistake of looking down. It was an awesome and terrifying sight. The wall seemed almost perpendicular, with nothing to break a fall. At the bottom were rocks scattered on bedrock and to fall on them would have been tragic.

There was no turning back. With Bubbud's encouragement, I kept climbing. I must not panic. Taking my time, I took one agonizing step up at a time. I reached forty feet. How could I have been so foolish as to believe I could run with this bunch? They had been born to this; I hadn't. I could not go on, but I could not go back either. One more step. Two. In great confusion, with my head spinning, I reached fifty feet. That was the end. I was stuck. If I tried to go higher, I would surely fall, perhaps to my death. As if sensing my peril somehow, Bubbud was suddenly there. He pressed me to the rock face with his muscular and powerful arms. I could feel his strength flowing into me. Together we climbed, and together we reached the top!

The view from the top was awe inspiring. We could take in the entire panorama of that cascading cataract, the pool of water at its base, and the entire river relentlessly rushing onward through the gorge below. Once I had gained my equilibrium, it was a simple hike to the hamlet we had set as our goal. Although the trip home was a two-hour hike, I hiked it willingly. No one could have convinced me to return down that shortcut into Tappia' Gully, and my friends, especially Bubbud, would not have let me past them anyway.

WHEN THE BRAKES FAILED IN BANAUE

It was sometimes necessary for us to go to Banaue, our market town, to buy supplies. In the market there we could usually get Chinese cabbage and sometimes beans and eggplant. We could also replenish our stock of flashlight batteries and buy kerosene in five-gallon cans for our lamp and stove. One time when I was in Banaue, I had bought our supplies and was ready to go home. The only jeepney I could find was overflowing, with people crammed into every available space.

Jeepneys are ingeniously remodeled jeeps used as public utility passenger vehicles. The front seat where the driver sits is a bench that can seat at least two passengers as well as the driver. There are no doors on either side. Sometimes a passenger will sit on the left of the driver, barely hanging on. Behind are two benches, running parallel to the length of the jeepney, which can accommodate from eight passengers to as many as those sitting will tolerate. Passengers enter the back of the jeepney from the rear. There is also no rear door.

Passengers on either side behind the driver of this jeepney that I was trying to ride on were sitting with other passengers on their laps and with their supplies piled between the two rows of people. People and cargo were even on the roof of the jeepney. Nonetheless, there was room for just one more to squeeze in if I was willing to sit on my supplies at the very back facing backward. I had no choice because I had no other way to get home. I added my things to theirs and was able to squeeze in my kerosene can, which I sat on. We started out. As we left the market area, the road was narrow and wound steeply downward, with buildings on either side. There was a sharp corner at the bottom with a river and bridge.

We had barely started down the hill when we realized that we were in trouble. The driver pumped the brakes, but they had failed completely. The only solution was to shift into a low gear and allow the engine to lessen our speed. He shifted out of the gear he was in and tried unsuccessfully to put it into a lower gear. Now we were in neutral with no brakes, freewheeling down the steep and narrow road with a sharp curve and a bridge to navigate at the bottom. We would never make it.

As the jeepney gained speed, I had time to contemplate the alarming probability of a major accident. We would certainly not make the corner, which meant that we would plunge down a bank of some fifty feet into the rushing river. We went around one corner screeching and slanting at a precarious angle. I could not see where we were going, but I knew that the sharp corner and the river were rapidly approaching.

I prayed. I could not believe that this would be the way my missionary adventure would end. God had rescued me in the past, and I knew he could do it now, though I knew that this jeep would not just stop of its own accord. I could see nothing but the ground rushing away from us. There was a sudden swerve to the right, a long crunching sound intermingled with screams, and the jeep stopped just a few meters from the sharp curve. God had prepared for this near tragedy by having a long bank walled up with stones, Ifugao fashion, and had prompted the driver to run the right side of the jeepney into it so that it finally ground to a halt.

We were saved—but not without injury. Three people sitting on the right side of the jeepney were taken to the local hospital with serious but non-life-threatening injuries. I do not recall how I eventually got home that night, but I remember the overwhelming gratefulness I felt as I understood that God's protecting hand was on all of us that afternoon.

MARCELO'S AMBIVALENT FAITH

A few men from Batad had ventured out of the Batad Valley as far away as Baguio, a resort city over two hundred kilometers away to the southwest, but still in the mountains of Luzon. There they had worked in the Benguet gold mines. However, none had gone as far as Manila. Our living in Batad changed all that. They now had "family" living among them who in turn had "family" in Manila. This allowed them to consider going with us to Manila to seek employment. They were desperate for money, since livelihood in Batad provided no cash income for them at all. We were their sole source of income, and that was limited to hiring a few people to carry in our supplies. Performing occasional jobs for us and helping us with our linguistic projects also provided some additional work for our neighbors. As time went by, some began asking if we knew of job opportunities in Manila.

On one occasion, while out of Ifugao, we experienced some difficulties at our guesthouse in Manila. There was a fence around the property, but during the night one or more people had been either coming through the gate or over the fence and taking items, especially from the little radio shack where our radio man communicated with missionaries in outlying areas. One evening, someone staying at the guesthouse discovered a thief inside the property and chased him out the front gate. The following night, some of the men staying at the guesthouse decided to stay up all night with the front gate unlocked to see if they might be more successful at catching the thief. However, the next morning, to their chagrin, a washing machine in an outside washing shed was missing! Obviously, while they were watching the front gate, the washing machine was being quietly lifted over the fence in another section of the property out of sight of the missionaries.

So the guesthouse manager decided that a night watchman was needed to guard the property. Yet where could he find someone both honest and conscientious who clearly had no Manila connections to tempt him to look the other way when things were being taken?

"I know of someone who would fit those qualifications," I offered. "The men from our village are completely honest, they have no connections with anyone in Manila, they are fearless, and they are extremely conscientious. I will be glad to bring someone down from Batad the next time I come to Manila."

Gahal was the first from Batad to work as a guard of our property in Manila. The loss of property abruptly stopped. The problem was solved. Gahal's fine work ethic and adaptability encouraged the hiring of three more men from Batad. Pag'i worked as gardener, Lucio as a carpenter, and Marcelo became the handyman around the house. Pag'i and Lucio, while still in Batad, had committed themselves to following the teachings of Jesus, which new believers called "the New Way;" Marcelo had not.

Mary, a retired telephone operator from California, had come to Manila to manage our guesthouse and did so with great efficiency. This was a place almost like a hotel for those of us who were living in remote areas. We could stay there when entering or preparing to leave the country, to care for immigration matters, get medical help, buy supplies, or just relax. Mary's heart was full of love and compassion for the Filipino staff who worked with her. Her desire to serve her staff came straight from a heart of love. She wanted to know everything about them—their needs, their joys, their sorrows, their problems, their walk with God. She constantly prayed with and for them and for their families. To get to know the Batad men better, she had made a trip with us to Batad. While there, she met many of our neighbors and friends, including Ilat and Inyap, Bon'og and Indang, Bubbud, Bugan, and many others. Her keen interest had enabled her to know a great deal about the Batad people.

Mary's special burden was for Marcelo. He was from a rich family and held many fields and rice wine jars, and as such had many responsibilities in the traditional Ifugao spiritual system. She talked with him and prayed with and for him constantly. On one occasion, when Billy Graham came to Manila, she decided that this would be a good opportunity to expose him to the claims of Christ. Along with the other staff members, Mary and Marcelo attended the Billy Graham evangelistic meeting. That night, Marcelo gave his heart to Jesus Christ.

Marcelo became diligent in his faith, reading an English Bible daily and enjoying Bible studies and discussing spiritual matters with the other staff members. We were greatly encouraged by his conversion, and we encouraged him whenever we came to Manila to read the Ifugao scriptures that we gave him. As far as we know, he never did.

However, the real test of Marcelo's faith came when he returned home for a vacation. Not only did he not associate himself with the little band of new believers there, but it was reported that he enthusiastically joined those still following the traditional religion in sacrificing chickens and pigs to demons. This was extremely puzzling to us and to the Batad new believers. He had shown such a remarkable spiritual turnaround in Manila. Had he forsaken his faith? We attempted to visit him, but whenever we went to his housing cluster, he was surprisingly absent. Back in Manila, Marcelo resumed reading his English Bible and joining with the others in spiritual activities. This conflicting and contradictory attitude persisted through several visits to Batad. Mary could not believe what was happening.

Finally, I was able to talk with Marcelo in Manila. He denied his change in Batad and explained that while he was there, his responsibilities were so numerous that he was unable to join with the new believers; his time was completely taken up. Eventually he quit his Manila job, went back to live in Batad, and took his place as a priest in the traditional system.

We tried to understand this contradiction. In the end, we came to believe that the problem lay in the fact that Marcelo had come to know the Lord in Manila and in English. True conversion involves a complete turnaround of one's life, body, soul, and spirit—psychologically, mentally, and socially. This means not only a transformation of one's relationship with God but also of one's relationships with other people.

It was relatively easy for Marcelo to make a decision to follow Christ in Manila. Those around him were Christians; they were pleased that he had made that decision. In Batad, however, the situation was vastly different. He was in a system that required blood sacrifice to the ancestral dead and to demons, and a decision to forsake that and to become an outcast among his family and friends was unthinkable. Although true and lasting conversions have taken place outside one's own culture, Marcelo's situation forcefully demonstrated the fact that the best environment for a person to make a decision to follow Christ is within his or her own culture. If he can stand there, chances are, by God's grace, he will be able to stand anywhere.

SKIN CANCER AND VITAMIN A

During the years we had lived and worked in Ifugao, we had spent countless hours tramping around our village and out to Dalican where we could get transportation to Banaue and Manila. I didn't like wearing hats, and so, for the most part, had been in the sun bareheaded. The prospect of cancer had never entered my mind. Eventually, I noticed a small lesion on my left cheek that simply would not heal.

During our next trip to Manila, I visited a doctor. When he saw the lesion, he immediately scheduled a time that he could remove it and send it off to a laboratory for testing. I waited several days after the surgery, and finally he called me back into his office to give me the results.

"The lesion I removed," he announced, "was cancerous. It was a carcinoma. I believe I completely removed it, but to be sure we should schedule several radiation treatments."

I was stunned! Cancer! I had no idea what it really was, and the name itself scared me. I asked the doctor whether it would spread, and he told me that a lesion like that would not spread to another site.

"Could it kill?" I asked.

"Yes, if left untreated."

"What can I do to prevent other lesions like this one?"

"Well, in the first place," he replied, "stay out of the sun as much as possible." He teased me, "You should have been born a mole!"

At that moment I was in no mood to laugh at his joke, though later I saw the humor in it. The doctor continued.

"You must cover your exposed skin when you go outside. You need a wide-brimmed hat, and you must always wear it when outdoors, even when the sun isn't shining."

"Isn't there medicine I could take," I wanted to know, "that would help protect my skin?"

"Well," he responded, "it would not hurt for you to take vitamin A. It is a vitamin that helps promote healthy skin."

On my way back to the home where we were staying in Manila, I felt discouraged. In my foolish mind, I reasoned that we had given our lives to the Lord to work to give his word to the Ifugao people, and this is the result. I thought, *What's the use? We might as well go back home where we would be safer.*

When I arrived, I told the bad news to Doreen. She too was troubled.

"Oh, by the way," she said, "we got a small package from the California church that has an interest in our work. Let's open it." There was an accompanying letter, which said that the ladies of the church had been cleaning out their missionary closet and had come across a bottle of vitamins. They packaged them up and sent them to us, hoping that they might be of some use. It was a huge bottle filled with vitamin A. I was completely rebuked. The Lord hadn't abandoned us after all. He just wanted us to trust him for our needs. Together, Doreen and I thanked him for his continued faithfulness.

DISCOURAGEMENT AND JOE'S VISION

For more than fourteen years we had worked in Ifugao and had seen very little spiritual awakening as a result of our efforts. No one had accepted Jesus as Savior and Guide through this life and into the next.

"If you will build your church here, we will all believe and follow you," several Ifugao had assured me. I was frustrated. I assured them that I had no intention of building *my* church here or anywhere else. I explained that I was from Canada, and there was a church there where we worshipped with many other people when we were there. If I wanted to worship in *my* church, I would go to Canada to do so. I had no desire for anyone to follow me. I was a follower of Jesus Christ. I had come here to give these people God's word so that they could decide for themselves if they wished to become followers of Jesus and build their own church in which to worship him. It was completely their decision. I would help and encourage them as much as I could, but I was neither establishing my church here nor a church to function under the direction of the organization to which my church back home belonged. If they were ever to have a church, they alone would make that decision; they would build it, and they would be in control of it.

It should not have surprised me that they would have this attitude. After all, anything from the outside had come to the Ifugao people as an institution without being decided by the Ifugao people themselves. The Philippine government—with their courts and appointed and elected civic leaders—the village leaders, and the schools and their teaching staffs had been decided by people from the outside. Even religion—represented by the Roman Catholic Church with its priests, nuns, and village catechists—came to them as a result of outside decisions. Outsiders had made the decisions to build chapels and church buildings, and the Ifugao people had been paid for any part they had in these constructions. The staffs and adherents of these institutions were all responsible to institutional control outside the village.

They fully expected that I, too, would fall into that category. When I did not, they did nothing to change their religious beliefs but continued to practice what they had done for centuries.

I was thoroughly discouraged. We had sent our children to a boarding school a thousand kilometers away, and we had worked, toiled, and waited fourteen long years for some indication of a spiritual response, and nothing had happened. I was ready to quit. I asked myself, *Are we just wasting our lives here?*

It was necessary for me to be in the United States for meetings, and I had the opportunity to visit my brother and his wife for a couple of days in California. My brother, Ches, was working on a project that produced the video process for recording and playing back moving images electronically through digital imagery. Moving images, of course, had been recorded for many years with movie cameras that used photographic film. This required the film to be developed and, if editing was to be done, to be cut into strips and pasted together. This new process, however, did not require photographic film at all. Images could be recorded electronically on recording tape and played back immediately or edited without cutting the tape. It was a major project that would revolutionize how movies, TV events, news, and so on would be recorded, stored, and played back on screens.

A video camera and playback equipment had been taken to the Soviet Union and were on display at the American National Exhibit in Moscow. The camera had recorded the "Kitchen Debate" between Richard Nixon and Nikita Khrushchev. Ches was telling me of these wonders, and, unknown to him, the more he talked, the more discouraged I became. Maybe if I had stayed home and undertaken something more useful, I too would have something to talk about.

The next morning, I was in his home alone after both Ches and his wife, Joyce, went off to work. The phone rang. A friend, Joe, was on the line. He and his wife and many others in California had prayed for our Philippine work and for us.

"Could I come over and spend time with you?" he asked. I agreed.

As we talked, I learned that he was not feeling well that day and had stayed home from work. As he rested, he told me, he had had what seemed like a vision. Now, I wasn't really into visions. I knew, of course, what the Bible said about them:

> In the last days, God says,
>
> I will pour out my Spirit on all people.
>
> Your sons and daughters will prophesy,
>
> your young men will see visions,
>
> your old men will dream dreams. (Acts 2:17)

I had had no experience with visions, and even though I believed in them in theory, I had to confess that I was a bit skeptical about them in practice. Anyway, I was ready to listen to what Joe had to say. He said that he had been resting and meditating that morning, and that what seemed to be a vision appeared before him. Whether he was awake or sleeping, he wasn't sure.

Before him he saw a vast country consisting of fold after fold of rugged mountains in deep shadow against a sky darkened by thick and thunderous clouds. It was a formidable sight, and he didn't know what to make of it. Certainly it was a place into which few would be willing to venture. However, as he watched, he saw the deep clouds gradually part, and a blazing shaft of light shine through. As it did, it lit up those mountain crests until they shone in the full force of sunlight.

That was it. That was his vision—somewhat terrifying at first, but then beautiful to view in the end.

"Did this sound anything like Ifugao?" Joe asked. "Do you think I have been witnessing the Ifugao ridges?" I fervently believed that he had.

We spent some time conjecturing about what it might mean. Surely the message was clear. Though Ifugao at present was engulfed in a dark cloud of fear, superstition, and oppression, there was the promise of a bright future. The light of the Gospel of Jesus Christ would surely break through to enlighten the hearts and souls of these people to whom we had committed our lives for service. My spirits rose. I was ready to throw off my pessimism and go back to work.

MOUNT AMUYAO ADVENTURE

From our veranda, Mount Amuyao loomed before me, commanding a gorgeous view of the far horizon to the north. It rose to a height of nearly nine thousand feet. I was told that to climb this mountain climbers could pass through the Ifugao villages of Cambulo and Pula, which would bring them to an elevation of about five thousand feet. With about four thousand feet left to climb, a climber would venture through an ancient and verdant forest before breaking out near the summit, which was often shrouded in fog. It seemed to beckon: "Come on, climb me!"

I could have given any number of reasons why I did not want to climb Amuyao, but I suppose most reasons could be boiled down to just one stubborn fact: it was a tough trip! We had tried to climb this mountain the previous year and had failed, mainly because of a combination of dense jungle, leeches, rain, lack of preparation, and not enough time.

This summer, my son Gordon and I were better prepared. We had to go! For one thing, since we had failed the previous summer, we felt we were obliged to redeem ourselves. Besides, I had not had a break since returning from North America the previous year. I knew that I needed a rest from my rigorous schedule. This trip would also give me time to be alone with Gordon. I felt this need keenly because he and Kathy were away so much during the school year.

In addition, our success would be a tremendous testimony to God's guidance and faithfulness. No one thought it could be done. Legends dating from antiquity related fearful things on that mountain: goblins, spooks, demons, and sheer rock cliffs. Legend had it that unknown forces could make you lose your way and cause nosebleeds and heart failure. We had heard it all. We knew that reaching the summit of Mount Amuyao would discredit the ancient views held by our neighbors. The absolute and fearful power of evil forces on the mountain would no longer have the same impact.

By this time, we had become part of the community and had close friends in the Batad community. We could surely find a few men willing to go with us. However, I noticed that no one seemed to be interested. Whenever we mentioned the possibility, the conversation quickly changed to other subjects. We had helped many of them in one way or another, though, and they owed us reciprocal help. Finally, after much persuasion, a few men agreed to go with us.

Gordon and I began to strategize our adventure. We wondered if we could climb Mount Amuyao in two days. The first day we could reach the village of Pula, high in the mountains, and camp overnight. We could climb the remaining four thousand feet to the summit the next day. If we hiked down at a steady pace without incident, we reckoned that we could descend back to Pula before nightfall. We would each need a backpack to carry our own supplies.

The stories and reports became more fearful and wilder as the time of our departure grew closer, until finally the day arrived. There Gordon and I were, ready to go, with our provisions and knapsacks, hats, and hiking boots. But there were no guides! Not one! One was sick, another suddenly realized that he had very pressing work that he must attend to, and others threw pretense to the wind and admitted that they were scared.

We had to start all over again talking them back into going. One argument above all others, I believe, finally gave some of them enough courage to agree to go. We assured them that undoubtedly the spirits are strong and fierce and can do terrible things, but that our God is supreme, and it is nothing for him to protect his children. We exercised our faith by assuring them that, as long as we were together as a group trusting God, no harm would come to us. God would protect us all. Finally Bon'og, Bubbud, Ilat, and Nattag agreed, very reluctantly, to climb that mountain with us.

They traipsed with us out of Batad, a sorry looking group with faces fit for a funeral procession. Gordon and I, on the other hand, were in good spirits. At least we were on our way! The first day was relatively easy. We followed narrow mountain paths, walked along the ribbons that bordered the rice terraces, scrambled over rocks, and crossed rivers.

We passed through Cambulo and reached Pula, the last village before Amuyao. There we secured another guide who knew Amuyao's lower regions like the palm of his hand. After a good night's rest in a little schoolhouse, the real work of climbing began. Almost immediately, we plunged into the jungle that covered the base and sides of Amuyao. Up, up, up we trekked. We held on to heavy vines to pull ourselves up. We clambered over or crawled under huge fallen logs, but we were always climbing. I was unprepared for just how grueling the climb had become. My breath came in gasps, and my chest heaved. We were climbing a nearly vertical wall, and without ropes.

One hour, two hours, three, four. How could I go on? Strange how a person will punish his body for such unnecessary reasons! We came upon a little shelf high up in the mountain. Then rest, sweet rest, while we sat and ate lunch.

How were we doing? About halfway up! What? Only halfway? How will we ever make it? It is remarkable how the human body restores itself. In half an hour, we were ready to climb again. I was stiff, now, with aching muscles. They complained, but after a quarter hour my tired muscles started cooperating again. We climbed over wild, tangled jungle vegetation that made climbing difficult and dangerous.

Then the first mishap occurred. Two men trailing behind didn't seem to be coming. We stopped, called, shouted—but no answer!

Oh God, please do not let them be lost. For your sake, let us find them quickly. In this jungle, one could be lost for days and perhaps never find his way out. Certainly we could not go on without them, so while we sat and waited, Bubbud retraced his steps down the mountainside again.

One guide voiced the fear they all shared. "An evil spirit has led the men astray as punishment for our invading his territory."

What could we say? We prayed.

In half an hour Bubbud was back. "They're coming! They took a wrong turn down below." Thank God. We were still all together as we headed off again.

Then Gordon started having trouble. A knee, twisted months ago and presumably healed, began to weaken. It was now five in the afternoon, and we could not afford to stop. We knew that we could not reach the top that night, but if we pressed on, we should be able to reach the top early the next morning. Gordon bravely kept climbing but was stumbling some. We decided to go as far as we could and then stop.

Dusk came. Gordon was exhausted, and I was looking for an excuse to stop, too. We found a small patch of level ground in the forest just big enough to pitch a tent. Hot biscuits cooked in a mess kit placed over hot coals tasted incredible. Night was soon upon us, and we felt the chill of the high mountain air. It's curious how peaceful and comfortable one can be in such wild country, snuggled into a sleeping bag beside a roaring fire. The stars spread out across the heavens, and the knowledge of a protecting Heavenly Father above lulled me to sleep that night.

At four in the morning, our guides were out scouting for water. How they could find a water supply in such wild country I'll never know, but they did. We made some good strong coffee, and we were off again. Breakfast would be celebrated at the top.

Our guide assured us that we could make it in two hours, and so we scrambled upward. The jungle had thinned out at this altitude. Trees were shorter ... a pine tree ... Then we came to a clearing, and the peak towered above us.

The final climb to the peak looked ominously steep. Up, up! We must be careful! One slip would be fatal. We were searching for toeholds and clawing the mountain face, grasping for any tufts of grass and small bushes that we could get our hands on. Eventually the mountaintop leveled off to a more horizontal plane. We had reached the summit!

We had made it! Gordon and I shook hands as our guides whooped for joy. As we prepared breakfast, two men gathered dead trees and branches from the stunted trees growing out of crags near the summit. With these, our companions built a huge fire. We needed a signal to prove to the whole of the Ifugao country sweeping below us that we had conquered Mount Amuyao. The men descended farther down the peak and, with little effort, brought back huge armloads of twigs with green leaves, which they threw on the fire. This sent huge columns of smoke billowing skyward.

In Batad, Doreen knew that we should be at the summit that morning. The weather was clear, and the peak stood out in all its glory. A group had gathered on our porch.

"They'll never make it," was the common opinion. Then, as they watched, they saw the smoke billowing skyward. It was a sign of God's faithfulness—a sign that faith in the God of Heaven can overcome the fiercest powers of the unknown world, even those of Mount Amuyao.

A FREE-FOR-ALL CONTACT SPORT

The village was abuzz with excitement. A water buffalo had been brought in over the treacherous trail clinging to the mountainside. There it was, staked to cross poles driven into the ground, tied securely, its neck resting on the cross. A sacrificial butchering was about to begin. Everyone was there: old people—some so feeble that they could hardly navigate the way to this rare event—, middle-aged folk, young people, children, and mothers with babies tied in carrying blankets. Doreen and I were there, too, with our neighbors, waiting with eager anticipation. Although we had never witnessed a water buffalo killing before, we were beginning to realize the magnitude of this event.

There was a slight stirring around the hapless creature. They were about to begin. We pressed forward with the crowd to get a better look. Bubbud, our Ifugao brother, waved us back.

"I will be completely occupied with looking out for Oltag and myself. There's no way I can also protect you. You'll have to go back to a higher terrace and view this from a distance," he said.

I felt a slight stirring of apprehension and alarm. What was this? Surely they would not become violent over the butchering of a single buffalo. Nevertheless, I trusted Bubbud and knew that he must have a good reason for not wanting us too close, so we cautiously retreated to a spot above.

A bolo was drawn. Its razor-sharp blade glistened in the noonday sun and seemed to be a signal for silence. The tumult dulled to a muffled murmur. With legs planted apart, the leader chosen as butcher for the task of killing and cutting up this beast had his bolo securely clasped in both hands. He raised it above his head, and, without hesitation, executed a rapid and resolute downward thrust. The animal slumped. Another chop, and a dozen men rushed in with tin cups to collect and drink a little of the fresh blood that was sure to increase their manliness.

With careful precision, the butcher now explained how he would dismember the beast. Each part that would be butchered was first announced and then assigned to a particular family. This detailed explanation, accompanied by much animated negotiation and gesticulation, began at the nose and ended with the tail. No part of the animal was omitted and no family was left out. When the procedure was complete, it seemed abundantly clear to all exactly which part of the animal each family would get. There would be no dispute about that.

So the butchering began. The butcher again took his bolo and, upon careful study of the motionless carcass, made his first cut. From the stillness of this mesmerizing moment came a plaintive objection: "That cut wasn't right! It should have been farther to the left."

The butcher paid absolutely no heed to this objection.

Another cut. This time there was a slight stir as two more unhappy men moved forward.

"That cut was wrong! Don't you know how to butcher a water buffalo?"

Again, there was no sign that this complaint had registered. A third cut and several men surged forward with bolos drawn pressing around the butcher, shouting objections, and waving wildly.

By the fourth cut, all semblance of order was lost as the entire mob descended on the hapless butcher and beast, each man bent on getting his share of meat. Suddenly there appeared a number of bolos entirely capable of hacking through any meat and bone that got in the way.

I was appalled; I was aghast. Had the entire village gone mad? Could no one shout for a semblance of order in the midst of this chaotic frenzy? The water buffalo was completely lost to sight. All I could see were the posteriors of determined men and women who pressed in. Wearing nothing but loincloths, these men presented an almost amusing picture. Occasionally, bolos flashed above heads, only to be lost again by the chopping motions of those determined not to miss out in exploiting this rare opportunity. I shuddered as I contemplated the wounds and possibly severed limbs that I would have to sew up when this was all over.

Suddenly someone broke from the crowd with a piece of meat clinging to a bone. Before he could get away with his prize, however, he was attacked by six or seven other men. There ensued a tug-of-war, the likes of which I had never witnessed. Screaming, clawing, pulling, twisting—each one tried vainly to gain their delicious share. The quarry was pulled this way and that, back and forth, until gradually the meat came off like hamburger, leaving nothing but a bare bone.

Time and time again, this scenario was repeated. However, it didn't always end in a pulling contest. On occasion, someone who had made an arrangement with two or three friends would emerge with a piece of bone and meat,; he would immediately throw it to his friend on a terrace above, who in turn would throw it to a higher terrace. The prized meat would be gone before anyone knew what had happened.

One elderly lady tried hopelessly to break through the tangle of bodies to reach the animal. No one gave the slightest notice to her presence. To gain attention, she grabbed a few reeds lying nearby and began pounding the backs of those on the perimeter of the mass. When this proved useless, she withdrew with the reeds and began flailing the ground and screaming in utter frustration.

Gradually I began to get a little insight into what was actually happening. This was not a village gone mad at all. Under the surface could be detected a carefully planned game. In fact, it was much like a rugby game back home in which players vie for a ball and are tackled and violently brought down unless they can break free of their opponents to either reach the goal or throw or kick the ball to someone else who can.

The event finally came to an end. The few who were left walked away from where the water buffalo had been. There on the ground where once the beast had lain was absolutely nothing but some partially digested feed and feces from the stomach of the animal, mixed with a little blood. Everything else would be cooked and eaten that night to celebrate this most unusual event.

THE CASE OF THE WALKING STAR

During our early years in Ifugao, talking with our friends consumed much of our time. We needed to know their language, and we needed to know it well. We could not learn it through study in a classroom or sitting at a desk. The only way we could learn was to sit with them for extended periods of time and talk and listen. I tend to be an introvert, so I found this part of our work wearying when it went on and on. At first, before I was able to follow rapid conversations, I would actually become dizzy and nauseated listening to the endless streams of strange sounds. Later, I enjoyed listening and sometimes participating in discussions, especially when they were of a cultural nature. However, I could only tolerate an hour or so of this before becoming mentally exhausted.

Many hours were spent sitting with my neighbors and conversing in their language about a wide range of cultural topics. Often I recorded the conversations.

One night we were sitting in a group discussing the events of the day. A glorious display of stars spanned the heavens, shimmering like a thousand diamonds in the moonless sky. They demanded our attention, and as we talked we admired this display of God's amazing handiwork. Stretched out across the dome above us was Aries, the Ram; the Big Dipper; Leo, the Lion; Orion, the Giant Hunter; and countless other constellations, most of which I could not identify. Our conversation gradually shifted to a comparison of their understanding of the heavens with our concepts of astronomy.

Someone began speaking of a "walking star." Others had seen it, too, and they began to speculate on what this strange phenomenon might mean. I was completely baffled. Some thought that this "walking star" might indicate that famine was coming to Ifugao. Immaya said that she had not only seen the star, but she had taken precaution against this bad omen by tying knots in the border grass around her sweet potato field. This would prevent an invasion of rats, wild pigs, or other predators from entering her field and destroying her crops.

What was this walking star? I thought that perhaps it was a comet or a meteor. The more they discussed its trajectory and speed, the more I realized that neither of these was what they were seeing. Then Limlim, pointing near the eastern horizon, exclaimed, "There it is! That's what we've been seeing."

What I saw was a very faint light. As we watched, it gradually climbed into the heavens and slowly passed overhead and down the western sky. I knew then that it was a man-made star—a satellite—shot into the sky to view either what was happening on earth or what was happening in the heavens. I did my best to explain what it was and why it was there, but it was difficult for them to take it in.

These were people frozen in time, in a period before the Industrial Revolution. The technological chasm between us and them didn't disturb me nearly as much as the spiritual chasm that separated us. We knew and had experienced the love of God and his message, but they groped like blind people in a world of demons and denizens of hell. The hopelessness of their search for comfort and relief was obvious as we observed their fear and dread of the unseen world.

INGGUHAD

Evenings were commonly spent in our living room relaxing and reading. We were always careful to have a large and varied supply of books so that we would not find ourselves with nothing to read.

One evening, Doreen and I were relaxing in our easy chairs with our books when there was a knock at our door. This was unusual, since by this time our neighbors would be asleep. I opened the door, and there stood a young man.

"Ingguhad is calling for you," he said with a worried look on his face. We considered Ingguhad our grandmother, though she had no close relationship to the family into which we had been adopted. She was an elderly woman, stooped and frail, but she still went daily to her sweet potato field on the mountain above our house. Each late afternoon she would return home and stop at our house for a drink of ice-cold water. She loved to talk and chew betel nut. She would exchange a box of our matches for a couple of her huge and robust sweet potatoes, which we found delicious. We would boil these potatoes and serve them like we would Irish potatoes, mashed, fried, or made into casseroles. In this way, we became intimately acquainted with Ingguhad. We loved her as we would our own grandmother.

Rice terraces, although they dominate the Batad landscape, barely provide a third of the Ifugao diet. Sweet potatoes are the main crop, carried here in a rain basket, which can also be used as a cape hanging down the back to keep off rain.

Ingguhad had not gone to her field for more than a week. What could she want at this hour of the night? Perhaps it had something to do with the ugly ulcerous sore on her leg that I had been dressing for the past week. The sore seemed to resist all of my attempts to treat it with injections and topical medications. I wondered if perhaps she was in such pain that she wanted me to come and give her something that would provide her with relief. I hurriedly put a few things into my bag, grabbed a flashlight, and started down the treacherous path to her house. It had been raining, and the path was slippery. At one point I had to scramble down over slick sheet rock. I knew that one slip would cause me to tumble down and keep rolling until a tree or some other object stopped me.

As we entered Ingguhad's yard, we were met by a sad and solemn sight. A group of people had gathered under Ingguhad's house. A woman sat holding Ingguhad in the middle of the little cluster of people. Ingguhad was reclining in her arms with her wounded leg stretched out in front of her wrapped in one of our bandages. Ingguhad was not awake, and I could not tell if she was unconscious or only asleep. People were talking in hushed voices, which indicated that Ingguhad was probably in trouble.

"She has been asking for you," someone hastened to tell me, "but she's unconscious now." How could I help Ingguhad? And how could I help these people? As we had done many times before, I told them that God, the Supreme Being, loved Ingguhad, and he loved them. If they would put their trust in him, he would accept them, be their God, and remove their fear of death. I may as well have been talking to one of the huge boulders lying nearby. There was not a glimmer of comprehension or belief. They seemed to be locked into this horrible system of appeasement of demons.

Ingguhad revived, and immediately the one holding her assured her, "Bullay is here now. He'll protect you."

Protect her from what or whom? I had no such power, and at that moment I felt completely helpless. Ingguhad looked my way, and a faint smile crossed her face. We began to talk as we had done so many times while she sat on our porch. I wanted to hold her myself, to tell her all about that Good News that we had brought but still had not translated. I wanted to tell her that she too could put her trust in Jesus and be saved. I had told her this many times before, but it had remained a foreign message to her. Maybe it was something that I could believe in, but she could not.

Then suddenly she looked past me, over my shoulder. It was as though her heart had contracted in a spasm of sheer terror.

"They've come for me," she gasped. "They're behind you, Bullay, sitting on that fence. They've come to take me away."

I looked behind me. I could see the fence, but I could see nothing sitting on it. I had experienced nothing like it before.

"Bullay," she continued, "they're looking at you. They're pointing their fingers at you, and they're laughing at you!"

This was incredible! Could there be any reality to this? Could it be that she saw something that I could not see? If they were indeed there, why would they be pointing their fingers at me and laughing at me? It made no sense at that moment.

Later, when I had more time to reflect on that horrifying scene, I began to theorize what the situation could have been. For those of us who love and serve the Lord, I believe that, at the time of death, angels do come and usher us into his blessed presence. So maybe when unbelievers die, demons come, instead, to usher them into a place where they will live forever without God.

Still, why would they taunt me and laugh? On the other hand, why not? Our express purpose for leaving home and coming to Ifugao was to deliver to the people, through translation, the message that could give them life and hope. We felt that where Ingguhad was concerned, we had failed. These demons had won her soul. I would like to have reported that she did eventually accept Jesus as her Savior and Lord, but she didn't recover from that horrible ulcer. She died soon after that night without hope and without God. This spurred us on to fully exert our efforts to translate the message for our neighbors and friends.

VIOLENCE AND HEADHUNTING

Ifugao people live in a hostile environment, and it was not uncommon for us to be involved in violent happenings within the village. The rugged terrain caused our neighbors to be constantly involved in perilous accidents.

One morning, we awoke to find a man on our veranda covered in blood, the result of a nasty fall from a terrace wall. His head was swathed in a dirty cloth, under which pounded leaves had been packed into a huge, gaping head wound. The dressing was a vain attempt to stem the bloody flow. His split head had the appearance of a dropped pumpkin. Despite its appearance, however, it was not a serious wound. Only the flesh had been split open. Although no bone was broken, it bled profusely. I worked for an hour or more shaving his head and cleaning and closing the wound before we sent him away as good as new. This was a typical accident attributed to malevolent spirits who push, pull, and shove their victims and throw stones or roll logs down on them. It is not infrequent that some die as a result of these accidents.

Other people suffered at the hands of fellow villagers. One evening, after our day's work was done and we had enjoyed a relaxing evening meal, we settled into our easy chairs for quiet reading and relaxation only to be interrupted by frantic pounding on our door. I opened the door, and there before us stood Mannong and two companions. Each man was completely covered with mud, dripping with blood, and trembling in fear and great agitation. It was a shocking sight. They staggered inside, and we quickly closed and locked the door.

There followed a fantastic tale of a drunken brawl with Nattag in one of the rice fields. We could imagine the screaming and struggling and the drawn bolos flashing in the moonlight. Their bloody bolos, now sheathed, confirmed their dreadful description of the evening's events. Along with cuts and abrasions on their upper bodies and hands, Mannong had suffered an ugly, six-inch gash on his arm. I had not yet graduated to the use of sutures, so it was necessary to make extensive use of butterfly bandages. These we fashioned from short strips of adhesive tape with small sections at the center covered to prevent the bandages from sticking to the cut. We patched up Mannong's arm wound with dozens of these homemade bandages. We used several more on the rest of his wounds and on the wounds of the other men. They spent the rest of the night in the refuge of our home.

Early the next morning, we hiked down to Nattag's house. The ladder was drawn, and the tiny door was securely closed and barred. We could only guess that Nattag, now sober, sat inside, trembling in fear of retribution. Nattag's neighbors made no attempt to hide their total satisfaction with this situation. Certainly it was a nice piece of poetic justice if ever there was one.

"Nattag," I began, "are you in there?"

A plaintive voice answered. "Yes, I'm here, but I'm not coming out."

"It's alright," I assured him. "No one will harm you. You know that I won't let anything happen to you. I want to dress your wounds."

Slowly the door was unbarred, and a pair of half-closed, puffy eyes peered out dubiously.

Again, I tried to assure him. "Do not be afraid. Mannong and the others are just as afraid as you are. You can come out now."

With much painful effort, he drew back the door, leaned the ladder against the notches in the bottom of the doorway, and slowly backed down to face his unfriendly fellow villagers. His pallid face was swollen, and one cheek sustained a nasty slash that lay open and oozing blood. As I patched him up, I emphasized the need for Nattag and his neighbors to live in peace with each other. When I had finished, I returned home, leaving Nattag and his neighbors the task of making peace with each other.

Divination by egg balancing on flat side of bolo

A casual observer of Ifugao custom would probably not suspect that head-hunting is still practiced. Although there is still much mistrust of traditionally hostile villages among some Ifugaos, no evidence exists to suggest that there are open or even covert belligerent acts of aggression. The American government, during colonial times, and later the Philippine government have effectively put an end to intertribal warfare and ritual taking of human heads for sacrifice to demons. Except for rare situations in which a human head is taken, the practice of headhunting lives on in an altered form.

As our neighbors' trust and confidence in us grew, we gradually became involved in the most intimate details of their lives. One day we sat with Munhin, a native priest, as he attempted to balance an egg on its pointed end, all the while reciting the names of evil spirits. The name he mentioned as the egg stood on end, he told us, was the spirit that had pushed Maladyu down as she carried a heavy load of sweet potatoes, smashing her face into a stone wall.

Maladyu's husband had died just a few weeks previously, and she was still distressed, so her mind was preoccupied when she fell. Along with numerous facial cuts, the fall had split open her lower lip and torn it away from her jaw. By this time we had graduated to using suturing materials to close wounds. We had received no formal or even informal training by a medical doctor. We simply copied what we had seen medical people do. To repair this damage, we sutured the wound inside her mouth with dissolvable stitching material and closed her lip wound and other wounds with stitches on the outside.

Maladyu's family felt it necessary to seek an appeasement of the demon that caused her accident, to avoid violent happenings in the future. Munhin contacted two other priests, and they prepared for the ritual that would include taking a human head. They agreed that we could accompany them on their foray into the forest. This provided us with a rare opportunity to view just how they did this without running afoul of the outside government.

The three priests set out early in the morning regaled in loincloths and ceremonial shell belts hung with scabbards and sheathed bolos. In one hand, each held a *bangkaw*, a type of fighting spear with sharp blades. These spears were without barbs to allow the blade to be easily withdrawn from a victim and used again immediately. In the other hand, the men held shields to protect them from the spears or bolos of their enemies. Doreen and I stumbled along as best we could with cameras and walking sticks. The group left a narrow trail, and we began our climb into the dense forest. We did our best to keep our walking sticks from becoming entangled in the dense and tangled vegetation, which would have immediately indicated our naïveté in negotiating forest terrain.

In a partial clearing near a ridge, the Ifugao men took out their bolos and began chopping away the tangled vegetation, trimming and setting aside some of the poles they were cutting down. Finally, they began erecting a house, a simple single-slant roof with walls of poles stuck into the soft forest soil. They proceeded to make a simple stick man using a vine to tie together two short poles in the shape of a cross. Grass was rounded into the shape of a head, and this was tied onto the top end of the vertical pole. When they were satisfied with their creation, they planted their man in his house and went off to enact the taking of this unfortunate man's head.

They first discussed the part each man would play and then set out to stalk and surprise their victim. Munhin went first, followed by Maggang—who was designated to protect Munhin—with Limlim at the rear to protect them from enemies coming up from behind. Crouching, carefully avoiding stepping on twigs or dried leaves, they moved forward as silently as possible, shields in front and spears at the ready. This was no joke. It was not playacting. These men were dead serious, and they were aware that their enemy, though unseen, was real. The enemy was the malevolent spirit that now possessed the stick man they had made. When they had approached the house, they paused, took a few steps backward, and then moved forward again.

Suddenly, Munhin, still crouching to hide his body behind his shield, thrust his spear into the body of the stick man. Maggang rushed forward to protect him, holding his shield while Munhin drew his bolo and lopped off the head of the enemy. He quickly put the head into Maggang's deerskin backpack. Slowly they backed away, still facing their enemy's house, holding their shields to protect themselves from the vicious spirit.

Further down the mountainside, they washed off in a small stream and began making head, arm, and leg bands. They made the bands from the white inner bark of the *hu'a* tree. Blood red terminal tufts of the ti plant, signifying death, were fastened to either side of each headband. Streamers were cut into the long ends of the arm and leg bands, which could then be tied around upper arms and calves.

With the headdress and arm and leg bands in place, they now approached the village. Standing on a promontory overlooking a housing cluster, they made a ritualistic announcement that they had triumphed in taking an enemy's head. Three times, in unison, each man thrust forward one leg, drew it back, and they bowed and shouted a mighty victory cry. A faint shiver ran down my spine as I pictured brave men enacting this ritual through dateless centuries coming home victorious from headhunting incursions into hostile territories.

At one of the houses, the priests removed their regalia. Inside the house they set out the severed head, a Ming jar with rice wine, a decorative wooden bowl full of rice wine, the house's protective altar box with bones and betel nuts sprinkled with the blood of previous sacrifices, three brass gongs, and chickens with feet tied ready for sacrifice. Prayers then began to numerous spirits, and especially to the spirit for whom they were performing this ritual. They beseeched him and the other spirits to accept this head and the sacrificial chickens as an appeasement of their wrath. They prayed that no more violent happenings would befall this family.

Sacrifice to the spirits was completed. Munhin and the priests divided up the meat for the family and close relatives of the woman who had suffered this violent attack and went outside to join a crowd that was gathering for a traditional dance. The severed head of their enemy was placed on a prominent post for display, and dancing began. The entire village joined in, dancing until the early hours of morning. The wrath of the Philippine government had been avoided, but our neighbors still did not understand that there was another God to whom they would surely give account when this life ended. This one could provide release and refuge from bondage to these devilish deities.

SEEKING AND FINDING THE WORLD OF DEMONS

It might be thought that it is grossly unfair that Ifugao people, without a chance to know the true God or his message, would be condemned to eternity without him. This teaching, which seems to be based on what is found in the Bible, has bothered me through the years.

Bon'og, a believer himself, posed this question to me one day. "What about my grandparents and other ancestors? They had no chance to know about Jesus. Should they be condemned to hell forever?" I have never heard an answer to this question that completely satisfies me. There are, however, a couple of facts that seem to suggest possible answers.

As we became intimately involved with our Ifugao friends, one stark fact involving the spiritual world became clear to us. The Ifugao people, and especially Ifugao priests, knew far more about that world than we did. They had made it their life's goal to know and relate to hundreds of spiritual beings, most of whom were evil. The priests' knowledge was not just of a general nature. They knew the gods individually and intimately. They knew them by gender, name, and personality, and they talked to their gods constantly through mediums. The

Ifugao argued with them, made bargains with them, placated them, prayed ritual prayers to them, and offered sacrifices to them.

Their knowledge, of course, was not completely accurate. Demons lie and try to lead those who interact with them astray. Yet one thing clearly stood out through all of this: the Ifugao knew about demons because they had set out to do so. They had made every attempt to know and interact with them.

When we asked them why they had not attempted to know about the true God, they invariably answered, "Because you say he is a good god. We do not pay attention to good gods because that would be a waste of our time and resources. If they are good, they will not do us harm. We pay attention to evil gods because they are the ones who can afflict us with calamity, sickness, and death. We need to talk to them and placate them so that they will leave us alone."

This led me to believe that if they really wanted to know the true God intimately, they could have known him in some fashion. How this would come about, I did not know.

A second and related consideration was that there were people who long to know and follow the true God, even though they knew nothing of his word. Mahhig was such a one. He was an old man when we arrived in Batad. He was a fine, stalwart, and honest Ifugao, and he did not practice the traditional sacrificial system. He had heard of God and had tried to follow him, though he knew nothing of Jesus Christ. He died before we were able to translate the New Testament. Will we see him in heaven? Only God and those who have gone on before us know that. Some day we will all know the answer to this question.

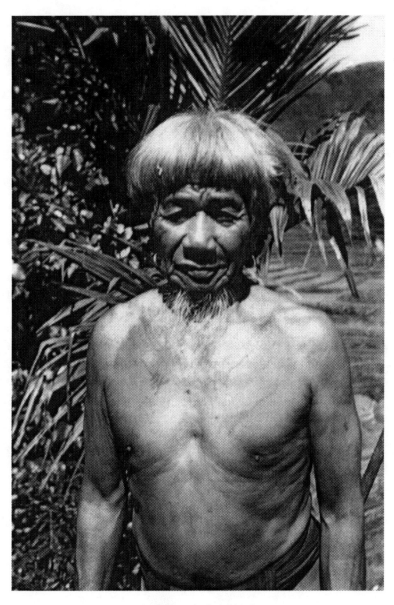

Mahhig, our dear friend

SATAN'S MIRACLES

Demons held a death grip on our neighbors. Daily evidence of the presence and power of the unseen world fortified this hold on them. Whenever prayers were offered to a sun god, proof that the god had possessed the body of a priest was baffling and beyond explanation. The priest possessed by one of these spirits would look directly into the blazing sun, wide-eyed, for as much as ten minutes with no sign of damage to the retina of his eyes. To those who cited this as an example of the power of the sun gods, we were unable to explain how this could be accomplished without supernatural intervention.

One day, we noticed smoke billowing from a cluster of houses in the hamlet of Hu'ab. This fire was much too large to be just someone burning trash. It was obvious that houses were on fire. Traditional houses were made of wood with grass roofs and were nothing but tinderboxes when fires start.

We ran down the path. Beginning at a spring and stretching up to Hu'ab was a string of people with buckets. They passed the buckets of water up the line to five houses that were burning. The water was dashed on the fire, but they might as well have been using thimbles for all the good it was doing. The blaze was so intense that the water had no effect on the conflagration. We watched helplessly as the five houses quickly burned to the ground. Other houses nearby, however, were spared by the efforts of people who wet them down by pouring water on them.

The loss of a house was indeed sad. Houses were built in a way that they could be disassembled and moved, and these houses had undoubtedly been moved many times. Some were so old that there was no history of when they had been built or by whom. They had come down to the present owners from centuries past. Now they lay in ashes.

As the ashes began to cool, the owners picked through the remains for something that might be salvaged. They came upon metal spoons that were rendered useless by the intense heat. Metal containers were also mostly useless and were thrown back into the littered piles of ashes. Someone kicked something in the ashes that was still intact. He brushed away the ashes that hid it from view and picked it up. It was an altar box, not burned or even scorched!

"Look!" exclaimed the man, carefully holding the altar box in both hands. "This spirit has protected his home from destruction!"

What could we say? Unless someone had surreptitiously slipped the altar box among the ashes when no one was watching, there seemed to be no natural explanation. With dozens of people constantly milling around, this seemed unlikely.

We added this event to our experiences pointing to the power of the demonic world to maintain control over our friends.

AKINU, GOLLANG, AND DEMON POSSESSION

Priests invited spirits of various classes to possess their bodies. At these times, the priests act as mediums through which the spirits could communicate with the people holding a religious ceremony. The priests invited this possession at these times for specific purposes and for short periods of time. If someone was ill, or if there was a specific problem that needed resolution, possession would occur. Permanent or even temporary possession at any other time was considered extremely evil and was avoided at all costs.

Akinu and Magyan, though not closely related to us, were our close friends. They lived in Ti"id. Gollang, their daughter, was mentally unstable; they said that she was permanently possessed by a vicious demon. We had discussed Gollang's problem with her parents many times. If it truly was a demon or demons that possessed Gollang's body, we knew that the best chance of a lasting solution to the problem would be for the family to become followers of Jesus Christ. They were, however, still very much involved in the traditional sacrificial system.

In fact, one day we happened to be in Ti"id and came upon a sacrificial event in progress at the house of Akinu and Magyan. Someone informed us that the occasion was the sacrifice of a pig to the demon possessing Gollang. The priests sat around in a close circle with Akinu, Magyan, and Gollang nearby. Displayed before the priests were the tools of their trade. An altar box lay open to receive offerings for the house spirit. A rice wine jar with rice wine inside stood nearby, and a little coconut dipper floated in an ornately carved wooden bowl. On one side of the room was a large pig with all four feet tied securely together. The priests quietly discussed among themselves what prayers each would recite and who would be the one to call the ancestors of the family to this event.

One priest took the dipper, dipped rice wine from the bowl, drank, passed the dipper to the priest on his right, and began to chant. The second priest drank from the dipper, passed the dipper along, and began chanting. This continued until all the priests were chanting their prayers.

Standing somewhat back from the circle, we observed this event much as we had scores of others like it. Then, without warning, Gollang frenziedly ran into the circle of the praying men, screaming and tearing at her hair. We could not understand the words she was screaming. Her father, Akinu, rushed in, held Gollang by her shoulders, looked into her face, and shouted—not to Gollang but to the spirit possessing her body.

"What do you want? What are you asking?" he asked desperately. "Why are you torturing us? Tell us what you want, and we'll give it to you." A husky male voice replied, but we could make out nothing of what was said. We had seen and heard enough and decided to leave. Unfortunately, this family was one of the few that resisted the Gospel we brought. As far as we know, Gollang was never relieved of her affliction.

4

MEDICAL WORK

CURING THE SICK

As we lived among our Batad friends, our ability to successfully treat sick people gradually became known. We had not come to Batad to practice medicine, and we had expected to do nothing more than a little first-aid medical work. However, the more first aid we administered, the more sick people were brought to us, and eventually we were attempting to cope with their most difficult medical needs. In fact, we were virtually their only source of medical help. We had tried unsuccessfully to have our neighbors take their medical needs to Banaue, fifteen kilometers away, to the missionary doctor there. However, they were unwilling to do this. They knew us, and they trusted us. In fact, at times when they sustained cuts and bruises in Banaue, instead of having the wounds taken care of there by a doctor, they would bring them home for us to care for. Fortunately for us, we had daily contact with a medical doctor on our shortwave radio whom we could consult on a daily basis if necessary.

It was true that we were generally successful in our medical work, but we were becoming increasingly preoccupied with it. We needed a helper. Carmen was a young Batad lady who expressed an interest in working with us. So we hired Carmen to dispense simple medicines, such as aspirin and worm medicines. She was instructed to call us for more serious illnesses. We largely attributed our successes to the guidance of the one we served. Certainly our successes in this area allowed us to be completely accepted, not only by those close to us but by the community at large.

Pneumonia and bronchitis among children was a common ailment. Often parents would bring their children to us with burning fevers. A mother would hand over her baby to us, and as we would take the little life in our arms, we could see the anxiety and apprehension disappear from her face. The concern would be transferred to us. At times we would be up with babies and young children all night, giving them steam baths to reduce their high fevers and make sure they survived. To the glory of God and his wonderful care, during the first several years of our work among the Ifugao people, not one baby brought to us for medical help died.

It was not uncommon for our friends to bring someone who had been bitten by a poisonous snake, usually on an arm or leg. This was often the result of picking up a large bundle of grass with a snake hiding inside. Immediately we would put a tourniquet above the wound and pack the limb in ice from the freezer compartment of our refrigerator. The swelling would eventually progress above the wound and we would put on another tourniquet and continue packing the limb in ice. This process of preventing the snakebite venom from traveling upward to the heart was repeated until we reached the end of the limb or until the swelling subsided. In this way, the body was gradually able to absorb the venom. Not a single one of our patients died as a result of snakebite.

One day we were brought a young boy who had been playing with a knife in the doorway of an Ifugao-style house without the ladder in place. He had fallen five feet to the ground below, and the handle of the knife had struck the ground, pushing the blade deep into the little fellow's neck near the esophagus. The parents rushed him to us with blood running down his neck and chest. We had never seen anything like this before. Could he possibly survive such a severe wound? What could we possibly do? Well, we could pray, and we did. We frantically leafed through our medical journal until we found the place where it discussed the anatomy of the neck area. We knew that the jugular vein was somewhere there, but we assumed that it had been missed, or he would have already bled to death. We finally satisfied ourselves that probably nothing vital had been cut. We carefully closed the exterior wound with some of our now-famous butterfly bandages, gave him an injection of penicillin and tetanus, and hoped for the best. In one week, he was running around playing as though nothing had happened.

In fact, we had become so successful in our medical work that people began to think that there was no limit to what we could do. One day someone came to us with a strange request indeed. Some men were attempting to bring a water buffalo into Batad. Along the way, the water buffalo had fallen off the trail and was lying in a gully some hundred feet below the trail. It had broken its hip and was unable to stand. If we had the proper injection, would we please come to where the water buffalo lay and give it an injection? They were confident that one of our miraculous injections would cure the water buffalo's hip and restore its ability to walk into Batad. They could hardly believe us when we explained with regret that we had no such medicine. They were forced to perform their religious ceremonies there below the trail in order to use the water buffalo to appease the spirits.

An important part of our medical work was to give smallpox vaccine injections. People of all ages would line up to get an injection. We gave these injections not only to our Batad neighbors but to people from surrounding villages who had heard what we were doing. Most had little or no idea why they were getting injections, but they trusted us for their physical well-being and were sure that the shots would help them. For months afterward, people would return with glowing reports of the strength of our medicines and how the injections had cured a vast variety of ailments.

One unfortunate effect of giving vaccine injections was that people would return to our little clinic, sometimes a year or so after having received an injection, requesting a repeat. They would describe their pains something like, "I had a pain here"—pointing to the chest—"and it traveled to my back and gave me pain all up and down my back. The injection you gave me cured the pain, but it has come back. So I need another injection."

We could try to explain the function of a vaccine injection as much as we liked, but sometimes it was useless. If we refused an injection, we would run the risk of being charged with withholding injections from them for reprehensible reasons. So, if all else failed, they would be given an injection of saline solution.

A STOMACH PUNCTURE

A young boy about nine years old was getting drinking water from the river. His family was poor so they did not have a water pail to use. Instead, they tied five or six beer bottles together around their necks, and these would be filled at the river and carried home. Being young and in a hurry, the young lad was skipping along over boulders at the river's edge, not looking carefully where he was going. He slipped and fell with the bottles between him and a rock he was jumping over. A bottle broke and cut a deep gash in his stomach just above the naval. It was a horrible puncture almost two inches long. With great effort he was able to drag himself home. His father quickly filled the wound with grass and leaves to prevent bleeding then carried the boy to us.

I took one look at the terrible laceration and realized that this was far too difficult for us to tackle in Batad. It would have been useless to tell the father to take his son to the missionary clinic in Banaue by himself. First of all, he would not have done it, but, besides this, I could see that the wound was already bulging dangerously and the little bit of stomach wall still containing the intestines would probably rupture before they could reach the Banaue clinic. I wound a long, wide bandage several times around the child's stomach as tightly as possible to completely cover and contain the bulging wound.

The only vehicle I had parked over the mountain was a small motorcycle, which we sometimes used for going to market in Banaue. There was an area of the road that was nothing but a flooded mud hole with no way around it. It was fully twenty feet long, and I had tried several times to plow through it on my motorcycle going and coming from market, only to have the motorcycle bog down in the middle of that mess. It would then be necessary to stand knee deep in thick, sticky mud, lift the motorcycle up as best I could, and literally drag it to the other side.

I knew that this little fellow was in critical condition. It seemed that there was no other choice but to take them to the clinic. So I asked the father, "If I go with you, can you hold your son behind me on the motorcycle until we reach the Banaue clinic?" The father agreed that he could, although he had never ridden on a motorcycle in his life. With that, the three of us set out.

The father hiked, cradling his son in his arms. Even with the heavy weight of his son carried in an awkward position, it was hard for me to keep up; this man was undoubtedly running on adrenaline. We reached the summit at Bolbol in record time and started down the other side to Dalican. There was no time that day to view or admire the luxuriant flora growing beside the path or to stop to cool off at the little stream along the way. Our minds were on one thing and one thing only; we had to get to the Banaue clinic as fast as possible.

We arrived at Dalican, and I quickly instructed the father how to be a passenger on a motorcycle. He climbed on behind me with his son still cradled in his arms. I drove slowly to enable him to stay on without holding on with his hands. He was only using his legs to balance himself and his son and to hang onto the motorcycle. His hands and arms were completely occupied with holding his precious cargo.

"OK," I announced, "here we go. Hang on as best you can." With that we started out.

The load behind me felt like a huge bag of rice placed upright. As we traveled along, the father swayed from side to side with no concept of helping to balance a two-wheeled vehicle. Although going was slow, we were making progress. When we were about halfway to Banaue, I thought that we might make it without incident, at least until we reached that terrible mud hole—how we would get through that, I had no idea.

Then, without warning, the father screamed out, "Oh, Bullay, my son is dying! My son is dying!" I looked back and saw what was distressing him. Below the tightly-wrapped bandage, the little boy's intestines were coming out. I immediately stopped the motorcycle, and the father and I got off. We laid the lad down on a grassy spot, and I began to work over him. The only thing that I could do was stuff the intestines back under the bandage as best I could and tighten the bandage even more.

Once they were completely contained under the bandage, I instructed the father, "Get back on and hold on with your son as best you can. We're going to fly to Banaue." Without concern for caution, we raced for the clinic, still at least three kilometers away.

The horrible mud hole was looming in the distance. As we approached it, I yelled to the father, "Hold on for your life!"

Praying with my eyes wide open, we hit that mud hole going at least fifty kilometers an hour. I had never been so reckless, and certainly not with such precious cargo! We fairly flew through the water and mud, hardly slowing down long enough to breathe. Miraculously, we made it to the other side and kept going.

At the clinic, the doctor informed me that his nurses had already gone home for the day, so I would be his nurse. We scrubbed up and started the operation, if it can be called that. After the doctor administered anesthesia, both of us began pushing and shoving, trying to get the intestines back into the body cavity. I was amazed at how much pressure there was against what we were battling to do. Finally, when it seemed that we had gotten the intestines all back inside, I held them there while the doctor sutured up the gaping wound. We were sweating and exhausted by the time we finished. The doctor looked up.

"We'll have to wait to see what kind of doctors we are. The intestines might have gone in straight, or they might have become kinked and twisted." I didn't want to think what the result would be if they were tangled.

Two weeks later, this young boy was again jumping over rocks, hardly remembering the terrible ordeal he had been through. He had no idea what his father and I had suffered on the fateful night of his injury.

DO NOT EAT YOUR BANDAGES

We were making good progress at language learning. However, when we made mistakes in the use of words or in grammar, we were hardly ever corrected. There were at least two reasons for this. We were from the outside world of "education and knowledge." We were experts, our friends thought, with anything that had to do with books or "desk" work. In fact, we were actually babes when it came to language learning, but many thought that our mistakes were somehow the result of our "superior knowledge." At times I would test Mannong to see if he would correct me if I made gross grammatical mistakes. I would make up a statement using grammar that I knew was wrong and ask him if what I had just said was correct.

"Yes," he would answer with a slight smile on his face, "if that's how you would like to say it." I could get nowhere trying to get him to give me an objective answer. In his mind, if I thought it was right, then it was right for me, even though I knew that neither he nor any other Ifugao would ever say something like that.

Another closely connected reason involves what Ifugao people refer to as shame. This is actually a matter of embarrassment or shyness to express an opinion that was contrary to that of some respected person. The concept of respect and deference is a strong value in the Ifugao culture and is difficult to overcome. In the early years of our language learning, we tried hard to get our friends to understand that we wanted to talk just like they did, and in order to do that we needed to be corrected when we said something that was not what an Ifugao would say. We tried hard not to show discouragement when we were corrected but to accept it graciously, praising them for their bravery. Bubbud was the first to begin overcoming the difficulties involved in correcting us.

One such occasion happened when we were working in our little clinic conducted on our veranda. From time to time, we received boxes filled with rolls of cloth prepared by ladies of a church in America. The ladies ripped white cloth into long strips, and we used hundreds of these rolls to bandage up wounds of all sorts. When someone would come with a cut on his or her arm, for example, we would dress it and carefully cover it with a bandage, which we would roll around the wound two or three times, pinning or sewing the end so it would not unwind. Ifugao people at that time wore little clothing and nothing on arms and legs. We would caution them, "*Adim anon nan du'upmu,*" which we thought meant "Do not remove your bandage."

The person with the bandage would smile and say, "*Oo, adi' anon nan du'up'u,*" which we thought meant, "Yes, I will not remove my bandage." Yet, as soon as the person was out of sight around the bend in the trail leading from our house, he or she would unwind the bandage from the wound and throw it to the side of the path. When we would go hiking along that trail, as we often did, we would see dozens of bandages strewn along the trail edge. They were not listening to our instructions, or so we thought.

One day, Doreen was in the clinic dispensing medicine and binding up wounds, and Bubbud was there with her. When she was finished bandaging up a boil on a man's leg, she repeated our admonition, *"Adim anon nan du'upmu."* Before the man had time to reply, Bubbud interjected.

"Kuyappi," he said, "you shouldn't say *'Adim anon nan du'upmu.'* You should say, *'Adim ānon nan du'upmu.'"*

"Why is that?" Doreen wanted to know, with a perplexed look on her face.

"The reason," Bubbud replied, "is that *'Adim ānon nan du'upmu,'* means 'Do not remove your bandage,' but *'Adim anon nan du'upmu,'* means 'Do not eat your bandage!'"

Of course those who received the bandages always promised that they would not eat their bandage! The difference was in the pronunciation of the word *"anon."* With the first syllable lengthened, the word means "remove," but without the lengthened first syllable it means "eat." That day we learned a lesson about the importance of paying attention to the length of vowels in this language.

A PATPAT VISIT

Batad is located in a huge bowl. Precipitous mountains border the basin on three sides and the Batad River cuts through it generally from north to south. We had very little inclination to leave Batad to explore other villages. There were two reasons for this. For one, even nearby villages were traditional enemies of the Batad people, and for another, the tremendous effort needed to hike up and down those steep inclines was more than we were willing to exert in the days when we were trying to learn this language.

The first reason was not true of the village of Patpat, however, which was situated over a mountain ridge to the east. The people of Batad had numerous relatives in Patpat. An adequate incentive to make the effort necessary for us to go there would require a reason of major importance. That day eventually came. Without vaccines, epidemics of major diseases were not uncommon. Batad and surrounding areas were experiencing a smallpox epidemic. To combat this, we had brought in anti-smallpox vaccine and had injected most children and some adults in Batad. We were told that smallpox was rampant in Patpat as well, and we were asked to go over to help them. Conveniently, I suppose, I had sprained an ankle and was unable to hike. Doreen agreed to go with Lab'an, one of the Batad ladies helping us, and they set out early in the morning. It was late that afternoon before they returned from their torturous trip to give me a report.

To say that the trip was torturous was no exaggeration. From our house, Doreen and Lab'an hiked down through rice fields, over and around huge boulders, and along narrow ledges to the river some one thousand feet below. There they carefully picked their way across the rushing river and up the other side. The far mountain swept upward two thousand feet to a narrow notch along the eastern ridge, a thousand feet above the level of our house. Hot summer days were upon us, and the mountainside lay dry and dusty in the scorching sun, broken only by steep slopes of shale, rocks, and thorn thickets.

Doreen and Lab'an slowly made their way upward, panting and perspiring in the thin mountain air. Halfway up, their water canteens ran dry, and before they reached the pass they were desperate to quench their thirst. There was not a drop of water on that mountainside. Over the ridge it was another five hundred feet down into Patpat. Doreen was anticipating people eager to welcome them in this mission of mercy, but it was not to be.

Word had preceded them that they were coming, and people were waiting in the small schoolyard to be given injections. They wanted this and nothing more. The village people offered no pleasantries and barely communicated with their visitors. Drinking water was provided only after Lab'an requested it. Doreen and Lab'an worked hard all day with no offer of a meal or refreshment of any kind. Babies and children were brought, many dehydrated and with high fevers. They desperately needed the attention of a medical doctor, but Doreen gave them what medicines she had brought with her. By midafternoon, they started their return trip up the five hundred foot climb to the summit, then down to the river and up again to our house.

When they arrived, Doreen was a sorry sight. Not only was she covered with perspiration but she was completely bedraggled and dusty and looked as though she was ready to collapse. Despite my sincere sympathy, I could not suppress a chuckle at her woebegone appearance. Doreen saw absolutely nothing to be amused at.

"They didn't give us anything to eat!" she gasped between huge gulps of air as she tried to get her breath. "They didn't even thank us!" My reply was more prophetic than I could possibly have imagined.

"They simply don't understand the situation," I explained. "They could not imagine that anyone making such a Herculean effort would do it without receiving huge amounts of money from the Philippine government, from the American government, or both. However, it will not always be this way. Someday they will understand." I did not know that within ten years there would be a spiritual revolution in the lives of the Patpat people and that they would welcome us with open arms.

DOREEN'S BATTLE

It was 1960 and time for a year's break from our work in Batad. No one had indicated much interest in the Gospel we had brought, but we had managed to translate the Gospel of Luke and two of the Pauline Epistles.

An anthropologist from Yale University had spent time studying agriculture in a nearby Ifugao village, and he invited me to apply for advanced study at Yale. I would study two years for a master's degree and then continue on for my doctoral degree if I qualified. My application was accepted, so for the next two years I studied at one of the best universities in America with all expenses paid for our entire family. My courses of study were in linguistics and anthropology, two subjects that I thought would best equip me for my continued work in linguistics and translation.

What seemed quite providential was the fact that a linguist had just come on staff from the University of California. He was a theoretical linguist and was in the process of developing a new linguistic theory that could be applied to parallel the work of others developing electronic devices for machine translation. I enthusiastically entered into this program. To me, it was refreshing to discover that someone in the field of linguistics was working to discover how both the meaning and the form of language could be analyzed and described. Almost all other theories were heavily oriented toward describing the structural features of language, with little or no reference to what these sequences of language mean. Eventually, I was asked to write an appendix to a book on this new theory that my professor was writing. I thoroughly enjoyed being able to discuss with and learn from some of the best minds in the world.

All was going well, and I was about halfway through my master's work when tragedy struck. Doreen, while working in the kitchen one afternoon, felt a definite lump in her stomach just where it touched the countertop. She didn't think too much of it at the time, but we decided she should have it checked out.

The swelling was an inflamed spleen, and tests indicated that she had acute leukemia. The blow was almost more than we could bear. We had just gotten into our translation project in the Philippines, and now this threatened to put a sudden end to it and to our happy marriage. What did the Lord have in mind with this?

I spent an afternoon with one of my professors, and we consulted his encyclopedias to learn as much as we could about the disease. One thing was certain: without direct intervention from above, Doreen would not make it. She would die. My professor friend made an astute observation.

"You know," he said, "the only difference between Doreen's situation and ours is that she has a pretty good idea how and when her life will end, and we do not. We are the same as she in that we know that someday, somehow, our lives will end."

I went back to our doctor, who practiced at one of the best medical institutions in America, the Yale-New Haven Hospital. He talked to me frankly about the disease.

"Your wife has acute leukemia," he said, "and, if she follows the normal progression of this disease, she has about two years to live." I then discussed our dilemma with the chairman of the department of linguistics.

"You are in the best possible situation under the circumstances," he assured me. "When your master's program is finished, you can enter a doctoral program and spend up to five more years fully supported by finances through the university." I went home and told Doreen what he had said. We prayed, we wept, we discussed our options, and then we prayed and wept some more. This could not be happening … yet it was.

Doreen didn't want to stay in New Haven. She wanted to return to the Philippines.

"If I only have two years to live," she said, "then I want to spend it with our adopted family in Ifugao."

"But Doreen," I said almost desperately, "how could we ever go back to Ifugao now? You know how difficult it is. It would be almost foolish to do that." I continued by pointing out our fortunate situation here. She knew all about that but still wanted to go back.

I ended up by saying, "Look, if we are to go back, we need to have a miracle from the Lord to indicate to us that this is what he wants, not just what we want." Doreen agreed to this, and we continued to pray.

We attended a church near New Haven that had never before practiced the injunction from James 5:14, 15a that says, "Is any one of you sick? He should call the elders of the church to pray over him and anoint him with oil in the name of the Lord. And the prayer offered in faith will make the sick person well." It may have been that they had not had an occasion when invoking that passage seemed necessary. In any case, they agreed to pray over Doreen and anoint her with oil, and to do that they called on a Pentecostal pastor to help out.

On our next visit to our doctor, he could find no swelling of her spleen and thorough tests were completely negative for leukemia. We knew that this was the miracle we had asked the Lord for, and from that time on I worked hard to finish my master's work so that we could return to Ifugao.

Time had come for those planning to enter a doctoral program to file their applications. Since we had already decided to return to the Philippines, I didn't include mine. The chairman of the Department of Linguistics called me to his office.

"Where's your application?" he wanted to know.

"I didn't file one," I answered, "because we plan to return to the Philippines at the end of this semester when my master's work will be finished." He was not pleased.

"Look," he remonstrated, "you do not know what might happen between now and the end of the semester. In any case, it will help to have been accepted now even if you plan to decline. You might want to reapply sometime later." With that, I applied for the Ph.D. program in linguistics and was accepted. I suppose I was one of the few who, after being accepted for advanced studies in such a prestigious university, declined to enter the program.

We returned to the Philippines in 1967 and immediately went back to work. Once a month Doreen needed to hike out of Batad to go to our market town, Banaue, to have her blood checked at the Good News Clinic. Each time she did, the results showed normal blood cells. We were overwhelmed by the goodness of the Lord in allowing us to continue working in this remote area. During the next five years, the hand of the Lord was on Doreen. There was no sign of the return of the disease. During these five years we completed an initial draft of the entire New Testament and three churches were formed, in Batad, where we lived, in Patpat and in Padyay.

5

THE TRANSLATION

AN IFUGAO ACCOUNT OF THE FLOOD

In the dim, distant past, the Ifugao people had exposure to some Old Testament accounts. These narratives, however, were never written down because writing and books were not part of the Ifugao culture, and so a writing system had never been developed. What they had were oral stories, passed from father to son or from mother to daughter. Because they were not written, the stories gradually changed from century to century, until finally they were hardly recognizable as a version of the original account.

One such story was an account of a world flood, which we know as Noah's flood, recorded in Genesis, chapters six through nine. There is an Ifugao version of this story told by parents to their children. What follows is a paraphrase of that story.

> Once upon a time there were two kings who ruled two kingdoms. One was King of the Land, and the other was King of the Sea. The two kingdoms were separated by a huge dike. On one side was dry land, and on the other side of the dike was the ocean. The King of the Land ruled over everything on land—people, animals, crawling and creeping things, in fact, everything that moved on land. The King of the Sea ruled over all of the fish, whales, sea monsters, and everything in the ocean that moved.
>
> Everything was fine, until one day, the King of the Sea noticed that some of his subjects had disappeared. He began to carefully investigate what was happening, and eventually he discovered that some of his subjects were being eaten by subjects of the King of the Land. So he called a conference with the King of the Land to present his grievances. The outcome was that the King of the Land promised to keep his subjects in check and that they would no longer eat any of the subjects of the King of the Sea. Nonetheless, the carnage continued. A large number of the subjects of the King of the Sea continued to be eaten.
>
> In a fury, the King of the Sea called another conference, this time yelling and shouting, "If you do not honor our agreement, I'm going to open the floodgates of the dike that separates my kingdom from yours! The ocean will spill over the land, and all of your subjects will be drowned!" Having delivered

his warning, he stormed off. Try as he might, the King of the Land was unable to control his subjects, since they had developed a craving to eat the subjects of the King of the Sea. Without warning, the King of the Sea opened the floodgates, and the ocean rushed through, covering the land.

The King of the Land ran for his life and was able to reach the peak of Mount Amuyao in Ifugao with a few of his subjects. The waters raged around them until the whole earth was covered except where they had taken refuge. All life on earth perished. As they waited on top of the mountain, the waters gradually receded. The King of the Land was anxious to come down from the mountain with the few subjects that had been able to reach the safety of the mountain with him, but he was afraid to venture down until he was assured that the land below the mountain had dried out. He eventually sent down a raven with instructions to find out if the land was dry. The raven never came back. It is a scavenger bird, and so when it saw all the bodies of those who had drowned, it stayed below and enjoyed eating the dead bodies. After waiting many days, when the raven didn't return, the King of the Land decided to send down another bird. This time he sent down a dove. The next day the dove returned with a small branch in its beak. This proved to the King of the Land that the land below was producing foliage again. He and his subjects made their way down the mountain and continued to live there. He blessed the dove, and that's why it has pink feet and a pink beak. He cursed the raven, and that's why it cries, "*Wak, wak!*"

THE TRANSLATION BEGINS

Ifugao folklore included many stories with obvious connections to accounts in the Old Testament scriptures, including the one about the great flood. However, all of them were changed and distorted in ways that make them useless in expressing God's word. Another such story was about a god who sent his son to live on earth. None of the rest of the story has any resemblance to the scriptural account of the coming of Jesus to this earth. Since this Asian culture, though complicated and highly developed, was not based on the Holy Scriptures, we felt an urgency to provide God's Word to the Ifugao people. It was for this purpose we had come, and so, with at least a rudimentary knowledge of this language, we began to translate in earnest.

The first Ifugao to work with us was Bubbud. It was appropriate that he would be the first, since he was the son-in-law of our father Mannung, married to our sister Oltag. He was a good speaker of the Ifugao language and proved to be of inestimable help in translating. He was also a farmer and thus was not always available to work with us. In addition, our work was so intense and so different to what Bubbud was accustomed to that he would often become mentally exhausted. We needed someone to help him. But whom? We considered surveying the available men of the village, but this would require a long and complicated process so, in the end, we prayed, asking God to send the one of his choice to help us.

Bon'og, Ifugao language expert and my faithful translation helper

Bubbud (right) provided excellent help in translating the New Testament. Ilat went on to become an excellent colporteur and evangelist to his own people.

One day, a young, very astute Ifugao priest, who was thoroughly involved in the ceremonial practices of the priesthood, came with his small son for medical help. His son was sick with a chest infection and needed medication. The father's name was Bon'og. We recalled seeing Bon'og on one other occasion when we were visiting one of the hamlets of Batad. He was sitting under his house dressed in a loincloth, chewing betel nut. He obviously hadn't bathed for a week or more, since he was dirty from head to foot, and his hair was tangled. He looked for all the world like a madman. We were accustomed to seeing men in this condition, since some situations involving the sacrifice of pigs required the priests not to bathe for extended periods of time.

Why Bon'og had brought his son to us was somewhat of a mystery, because a priest would be the last one to admit that sacrificing animals was not an effective method of curing illnesses. Bon'og admitted that they had already offered chickens and pigs to appease the gods, and still his son hadn't recovered. One of his neighbors urged him to bring his son to us, because there were many reports circulating of the power of our medicines to cure illnesses. Bon'og, however, had a problem. He had no money.

"Can I owe you for the cost of the medicines necessary to cure my son?" he asked.

We had just recently changed our practice in this regard. At first, we had allowed people to owe us for their medicines, only to find that they often did not return to pay off their debts. Eventually, we had a very long list of those owing us for medical services. An unfortunate result of this was that those owing for medicines would not return when they or a member of their family needed medicines again, because, except in emergency situations, they were required to pay off their debts before getting medicines a second time.

We were in a very difficult situation. On the one hand, we simply could not give out free medicines, since our medical practice was financially supported from our personal funds and we ourselves were required to live frugally. On the other hand, we knew that money in Batad was exceedingly scarce, and people became sick even though they had no money with which to pay for medical help. They did have their agricultural produce. They had sweet potatoes, rice, chickens, and sometimes a few vegetables or fish. So we adopted a policy of accepting food as payment.

We explained our policy to Bon'og, and his face fell. "I have nothing right now that I can give you as payment," he said. He was about to leave with his sick child when I had an idea.

"Listen, Bon'og," I suggested, "how about it if you work for me for one week, and over the period of that week I inject your son with a medicine that we hope will make him well?"

Bon'og was skeptical. "I am a priest; I know nothing of books."

"You do not need to know anything about books," I assured him. "All that is required is that you know your language."

As it turned out, Bon'og was a brilliant man. He had an amazing grasp of his own language and the culture in which he lived. By the end of the week his son was completely over his chest infection, and it had become clear that Bon'og would make an excellent helper in our project. He agreed to work with us.

DEMONS THAT "SPEAK IN TONGUES"

Bon'og and I were in a deep discussion of a translation problem at my translation desk. As we circled in on the probable meaning, a faint voice in the background finally penetrated my consciousness. It was Carmen, our helper in the clinic on the upper porch. She was calling for help. Carmen cared for the twenty to fifty people who came each day with medical problems. Only when she and Doreen were unable to cope with a situation was I called away from my translation desk to help. Judging from the urgency in Carmen's voice, this was one of those times.

I ran onto our veranda, where a number of people were sitting, waiting their turn for medical help. A middle-aged woman was sitting in some kind of distress with Carmen bending over her. As I approached, Carmen stepped back. The woman was in the throes of what appeared to be an epileptic fit. Her legs were extended, head thrown back, eyes open and glassy, face and body wracked in involuntary muscle spasms.

"Please move back," I requested, as people crowded in. "Give her room. Let me lay her down on the bench."

Thoughts raced through my mind as I tried to remember what to do with a person undergoing an epileptic attack. All I could think of was that she should be positioned so her tongue would not fall backward into her throat. All the while, Lab'an, our faithful cook, was watching at a distance from the kitchen. She was never reluctant to give advice in areas outside the kitchen when the situation warranted.

"No!" she cried. "Do not lay her down! She isn't sick. Sit her up! A spirit is taking possession of her body. It wants to talk to you!"

I was shocked. Could this be what was happening? Overt spirit activity was a daily occurrence in this village. Native priests continually acted as mediums for spirits demanding sacrifices of chickens and pigs. I had seen this and knew something of the spirits' powers and control over the lives of these superstitious people. Never before had a spirit attempted to talk to me directly.

While these thoughts raced through my mind, the woman stopped convulsing. She sat still with a glassy stare, looking directly at me. The hair on the nape of my neck bristled. Was this my imagination, induced by Lab'an's urgent shout?

The woman's husky voice broke through with a ring of challenge: "Why are you here? By what authority have you come?" I opened my mouth to answer. Yet my words did not come. I was stunned by the realization that this woman was speaking English—American English. It could not be happening. A Batad Ifugao woman could not be speaking American English. Yet she was! Then the truth of the situation finally penetrated my confused mind. A demon of hell was challenging our right to invade Satan's stronghold. Never before had this happened to us—never! Should I answer the demon? Should I engage this evil spirit in an argument?

All at once I felt a strong compulsion to avoid direct communication. The words of Revelation 12:11 took control of my thoughts: "They overcame [Satan] by the blood of the Lamb and by the word of their testimony."

Then I knew. I was to resist this demon on the authority of the blood of the Lamb.

"Dear Lord Jesus Christ," I prayed with my eyes open, fixed on the woman, "this poor woman is afflicted with a demon. Deliver her! On the authority of your word, I ask, free this woman. By the power of your shed blood when, through your sacrifice, you defeated Satan and all his cohorts, cause this demon to leave her!"

The woman slumped on the bench like a spent rocket. It was all over. The demon had gone. And, I thought, truly "our struggle is not against flesh and blood, but against the rulers, against the authorities, against the powers of this dark world and against the spiritual forces of evil in the heavenly realms." Ephesians 6:12.

A HEADHUNTING STORY

Again I was at my desk with more than a dozen open books propped in front of me. On the pages of the versions of the New Testament were devices that held the pages open to the page being translated; little bamboo sticks with rubber backing securely marked the exact spot on the page. Seven of the books were stacked on a kind of carousel that rotated on a central bearing, allowing for quick access to any of those references.

One of these books was a Greek New Testament that I used as my basic text. I had taught one Ifugao lady the Greek alphabet, and she had pulled three-by-five slips of the important words to be translated that day from file boxes which contained our Greek-to-Ifugao records. They lay beside me on my table. Beside me at another smaller table was Bon'og. During times when I was working alone, he was busy with other language work, writing out stories, checking a previous translation, compiling sets of related words from our dictionary file, or doing one of many other tasks.

It would undoubtedly have been an amusing and incongruous sight for any-one from the outside to look in on us at work—books everywhere, both of us stu-diously busy at what we were doing. A little bench was provided for Bon'og to use in working at his desk. He did not want a cushioned seat. Cushions were unknown in Ifugao. Nor did he sit on his little bench. There he was with no shirt, wearing only a loincloth. He squatted on his haunches, feet firmly planted on the bench, the "tail" of his loincloth falling down behind. Things were not as they appeared. Bon'og was just as expert as I in what he was doing, and far more expert in the use of his language. He was a veritable gold mine of information on Ifugao words and meaning. His work as an Ifugao priest had prepared him well for what he was doing.

While we were working there was a sudden, desperate cry from above our house. I could not catch what was said, but Bon'og did. With one leap he left his "perch," dashed out the door, ran upstairs two steps at a time, grabbed a spear I kept mostly for purposes of cultural interest, and rushed out the front door and up the hill on the trail we use for leaving the village. I didn't know what to make of this startling display of urgency. However, I had no intention of allowing an obvious tragedy to transpire without in some way being part of it. So I dropped my pen and ran after Bon'og. I soon saw that several other stalwart warriors, loin-cloth clad and also holding spears, were running along with Bon'og.

Someone caught up with me on the trail. "What's happening?" I gasped as I tried to get my breath.

"A woman is being beheaded in the fields above the trail," was the chilling response.

Could it be? Did I want to get involved in that? I had no armor, and even if I did I had no idea how to use it. Nor was I inclined to do so. While these things were rushing through my mind, I noticed that the men began to slow down and then stopped. Now what?

"False alarm," someone announced. No one was being beheaded after all. It was a case of mistaken communication. There were two ladies far up in their sweet potato fields and they needed help, but it was not to prevent being beheaded. One of their pigs had gotten into the fields and was destroying the crops. They needed help to catch it and bring it home. What an anticlimax! I thanked God that it was nothing more serious than a runaway pig. I realized that these people were still barely beyond the headhunting era.

TRANSLATING A STORY OF DEMON POSSESSION

At first, all went well as we translated with Bon'og's help. He was a quick learner. He soon began to grasp what we were trying to do. He didn't have the burden of knowing English or the English Bible to confuse him when trying to put into his language the intent of the writer of the New Testament book we were working on. His suggestions and phrasing of the word came from his deep knowledge of his language, of the sacrificial system of his religion, and of an artistic way of using the Ifugao language to express concepts. We were making excellent progress. We knew, though, that Satan would most definitely not allow us to continue undisturbed. We were translating Bible passages that challenged his power. As it turned out, he did indeed attempt to end Bon'og's participation in translating.

Seven years was required to produce a rough draft of the New Testament. Three more years were spent producing a manuscript ready for publication.

We were working on Luke 8, which tells of Jesus healing a demon-possessed man. When we were well into this account, a man came to my study asking for Bon'og.

"You must come home right away!" The man was insistent. "Something has come up and you are needed there."

The situation sounded urgent, although the man did not give us the reason. So Bon'og went home with the man. It was midafternoon, and when Bon'og did not return, I assumed that whatever he was needed for was taking him the rest of the afternoon. The next morning, he failed to come back to continue our work. I thought that perhaps someone in his family was sick and he was needed to look after them. Could his wife have fallen ill?

When Bon'og had not returned the third day, I decided I'd better go to his house to see what the problem was. He was there by himself puttering around at what seemed to me to be an unimportant task.

"What has happened?" I asked in a perplexed voice. "I have been waiting for you for the past two days." We sat on a log to talk and he described to me a bizarre tale.

"I won't be continuing my work with you," he began. He continued by telling me why he was called home and what had happened. When he arrived, he was surprised to discover a group of priests under his house already involved in sacrificing a chicken to some spirits. This was a complete surprise to Bon'og, since he had not called them, and he knew of no need for them to be there.

The priests informed him that they had been called by Indang, Bon'og's wife. She was ashamed to let Bon'og know what had happened to her. It seemed that she had been having dreams of being married to a demon, and he had had an intimate relationship with her. She had detested that and wanted to be free of this relationship. The only way to do this was through offering sacrifices of chickens to the spirit involved. When the spirit took possession of a medium priest, it informed them that it would not consider freeing the woman until her husband, Bon'og, was included in the circle of priests. That was the reason Bon'og was called. Being a priest himself, he sat with them.

After explaining the situation to him, they again began their chanted prayers. Without warning, Bon'og was possessed by the spirit that had had the relationship with Indang in her dreams. This was completely unexpected, and was, in fact, an unwanted and scary situation, since Bon'og had not agreed to have the spirit possess his body. When a spirit takes possession of the body of a priest, it is always with the permission of that priest. When the demon left his body, Bon'og was severely shaken.

What could all this mean? Then he remembered that he had been working with me on a Bible passage that spoke of a man who had been cured of demon possession. Obviously, this was a warning for him to have nothing more to do with this business of translating the Bible.

"Bon'og," I argued, "don't you see what is happening? Of course this demon or any other demon would not want you to work on the Bible, which tells of the power of Jesus over demons. If you had continued with me, you would have seen how Jesus had exorcised not just one demon but many demons that had possessed this man. He cast them out because there is no limit to his power. He will take care of you and your family if you will continue on with me to translate his word." At first Bon'og was skeptical, but in the end he did return and we completed that passage and went on to other Biblical accounts in the New Testament.

JESUS AND BEELZEBUB

We were translating and had reached the story of how Jesus had cast out a demon in Luke 11:14–20. In the story, some of the people conjectured that "By Beelzebub, the prince of demons, he is driving out demons." Jesus, knowing their thoughts, said, "Any kingdom divided against itself will be ruined, and a house divided against itself will fall." Why these two sentences were put side-by-side, Bon'og could not imagine. I was at a loss to explain why they made perfect sense to me. After a long discussion about this, I finally began to understand the problem. It had to do with our cultural differences, or, more accurately, the cultural difference between how a Greek or Hebrew would understand this passage and how an Ifugao would understand it. There was obviously information understood by a Greek or Hebrew but not stated that needed to be explicitly expressed for an Ifugao to understand this story.

I discovered that an Ifugao reading this would immediately say, "How clever of Jesus to use the power of Beelzebub to drive out demons! That's exactly what we would do." In fact, Ifugao priests commonly used the help of demons to drive out other demons from demon-possessed people. So their understanding was that if Jesus drove out demons by the power of Beelzebub, then good!

With that in mind, the statement, "Any kingdom divided against itself will be ruined, and a house divided against itself will fall," made no sense at all. We knew, of course, that it would not do for us to put in a whole paragraph to explain this cultural difference, but we could, perhaps, at least raise the question of it by the addition of one or two words. The subject would then need to be investigated and understood with further study of the New Testament and its cultural background. So we translated the passage somewhat as follows: "Some of them severely criticized Jesus, saying, 'By Beelzebub, the prince of demons, he is driving out demons.'" Our hope was that if this was stated as severe criticism and not praise, it would be a smaller jump to understand that this was the case among Greeks and Jews during Jesus' time on earth, even though it might be thought of as praise by an Ifugao.

6

THE CHURCH

GOD TALKS IFUGAO

As Doreen continued with her work making and testing primers and reading materials, I continued translating. I was becoming more proficient in explaining to Bon'og and Bubbud what the text was saying, and they were becoming increasingly more proficient in wording it in an accurate and natural way in their language. No one had yet believed this Message, as far as we were aware, despite the fact that it had been fully sixteen years from when we first entered Ifugao. I was beginning to wonder if the so-called vision that our friend Joe in California had had was just that—a "so-called" vision without any substance. Still, we hung on and continued our work, drawn by a hope that somehow something would eventually happen.

One day, when Bon'og was translating with me, he suddenly stopped and exclaimed, "Bullay, something very strange is happening to me."

"What is it?" I wanted to know.

He responded, "By now, you know the custom of married men and the sleeping houses of single girls." Indeed we did. It was perfectly fine for married men to interact intimately with single girls in their sleeping houses, provided the men's wives did not object. Bon'og continued.

"Since working on this book, which you call the word of God, I feel ashamed to go to the single girls' sleeping houses. In fact, I simply can't do it. You also know our custom that allows us to cut off a stock of sugarcane growing along the dikes and chew it to extract its juice when we're thirsty." Yes, I also knew about that practice. In fact I had been with some of them when they had done it. "Well," Bon'og continued, "when I begin to do that, there's something that seems to tell me that this is wrong. What is wrong with me? Am I becoming a non-Ifugao?" I smiled.

"No, Bon'og, you're not becoming a non-Ifugao—you're becoming a converted and changed Ifugao. You see, Bon'og, the book we're working on is a powerful book. As you work with me in translating this book, the Holy Spirit is working in your heart to let you know that there are some things in the Ifugao cultural system that displease God. When you begin to do things that displease God, the Holy Spirit reminds you of God's word and what he says about that. The Ifugao culture is not bad. It is a good culture, and you should follow it as much as you can. However, when you are aware of something in it that displeases God, because you have learned about that in his word, you should stay away from that."

Within a few days, as Bon'og and I continued to discuss these things, he bowed his head and heart and invited Jesus Christ into his life. We felt that it was completely appropriate that the first one to believe would be one of our helpers in translating the Bible.

Eventually, all three men who helped me in translating put their trust in Jesus Christ. It was relatively easy for them to understand the power of the word, since it had been as we translated it that they themselves came under conviction of their sins and trusted the Lord for their salvation.

This was especially true of Ilat. He was one of the very few men who had spent time away from Ifugao. He was a poor man with few fields and, consequently, without major responsibilities in the village, so he had sought employment outside his home province. During a time when he was in the province of Nueva Vizcaya, just out of Ifugao, he happened to come in contact with an Ilocano Methodist minister. Eventually Ilat moved in with the minister and his family for a period of time. Ilocano is the language commonly spoken in Nueva Vizcaya, and there is a translation of the Bible in that language. Yet, although he undoubtedly received a clear witness to the Gospel in the Ilocano language, he did not sense that the message he heard was speaking to him. It was not until he returned home and worked at the translation desk with me that the word began to penetrate his heart. Eventually he, too, accepted Christ into his life.

So it was without any urging or suggestion on my part that these three men felt they should share the Message of the Bible with their families and friends. They would often take copies of the typewritten New Testament manuscripts home with them. They would kindle a little fire under their houses for light, gather their families and neighbors around, and begin reading the translated scripture portions. They were so anxious to share the Message that when they had exhausted reading the typewritten portions, at the end of a day of translating they would take the written manuscripts from my desk to read at home. I was somewhat anxious when this happened, but the manuscripts always came back the next day.

There were times when, out of curiosity, Doreen and I would go into a hamlet where one of my helpers lived to sit and listen to them reading the scriptures. Often there would be twenty or thirty people gathered. The reader would sit with the paper so close to the fire that I would be afraid it might catch fire. As the word was read, there was complete silence, except perhaps for the whimper of a child sleeping on the back of his mother. Those who gathered seemed to hang on every word. I had rarely seen people in church back home pay such close attention when the Bible was read. At the end, those who listened would begin asking questions and commenting on what they had heard.

On one such occasion, when the people began to disperse after a reading, an Ifugao priest came to me.

"It was just as though God was talking to us!" he said with amazement in his eyes.

"He was." I answered. "You see, what was read is God's word. He now speaks to you because God now speaks your language through what is written in Ifugao."

Only then did we begin to understand what was happening. Before, we had told them as best we could of God's love, of his death and resurrection, which could ransom them from their sins. We told them that if they would put their trust in him, they would live with him forever. They sensed that this might be true for us, but that it was different for an Ifugao. Their system required them to follow the ways of their ancestors. However, now it was different! It was no longer an outsider coming to them trying to tell them what God was saying. It was God himself talking to them! This initiated the birth of the infant Ifugao Church.

AN ANGRY GOD

Each language has one or more cultural keys that unlock the door to the reception of the Gospel message. In Ifugao, we were continually looking for something within God's word that would spark a fire of receptivity. The idea of a loving God who would guard and protect his children seemed to us to be a message that would appeal to our friends and Ifugao family. For centuries, the Ifugao people had lived lives of fear and dread of spiritual forces arrayed against them. We had agonized with them as we saw them attempt to appease angry demons. We thought that if only they could appreciate God's love, they would turn from sacrificing demons to follow and worship a loving God. So one of the first hymns we translated, "The Love of God," was about God's love:

The love of God is greater far
Than tongue or pen can ever tell.
It goes beyond the highest star
And reaches to the lowest hell.
The guilty pair, bowed down with care,
God gave his Son to win.
His erring child he reconciled and pardoned from his sin.

O love of God, how rich and pure,
How measureless and strong;
It shall forevermore endure,
The saints' and angels' song.

One of the earliest verses we translated was John 3:16, "God loved the people of this world so much that he gave his only Son, so that everyone who has faith in him will have eternal life and never really die." However, neither the song nor the verse seemed to have much effect on our friends, and we wondered why. Obviously whatever would move them to give up their slaughter of chickens and animals to appease demons would be God's doing and not ours.

What eventually proved to be a most convincing message was almost directly opposite to what we had predicted or even hoped would move them. As the first Ifugao villagers put their faith in Jesus Christ, they gave testimony to being greatly moved by verses such as Matthew 18: 6–9, which give a terrible warning:

"But if anyone causes one of these little ones who believe in me to sin, it would be better for him to have a large millstone hung around his neck and to be drowned in the depths of the sea.

"If your hand or your foot causes you to sin cut it off and throw it away. It is better for you to enter life maimed or crippled than to have two hands or two feet and be thrown into eternal fire. And if your eye causes you to sin, gouge it out and throw it away. It is better for you to enter life with one eye than to have two eyes and be thrown into the fire of hell."

The fact that the Creator of everything hated sin so much that he had prepared a terrible place for those who were guilty of sin and refused to follow him was a message that really made our friends think about what awaited them if they did not put their trust in God. They had come to realize that putting their trust in the Lord not only removed them from the curse of sin but put them under his loving care and protection. This new understanding helped them to truly appreciate God's love.

THE SEAL OF FAITH

We had already translated several passages about baptism, including the one in Acts 16, which tells of a jailer who had guarded Paul and Silas in prison but who had believed in the Lord Jesus Christ along with his family. The passage says that even though it was midnight, the jailer and his family were baptized.

There was now a small band of believers in Batad, and they began to ask about being baptized. They had no idea what this involved, but they seemed to equate it in some way with a traditional Ifugao ceremony that commits their children to the care and protection of spirits. They saw baptism as a public act that would seal their faith. Being baptized would declare that they had forsaken a religion based on appeasement of demons and had embraced one of faith in God and his Son, Jesus Christ.

After much discussion about this—during which we read together all the scripture translated to date on this subject—one of the questions was how exactly baptism should be performed. We told them that there were two main methods of doing this. Some believers had water sprinkled on them, while others were immersed in water. We went on to explain the symbolism of both methods and explained, as best we could, the advantages and disadvantages of both methods. We naïvely thought that by being as general and unbiased as possible, we could avoid influencing their decision about the method they would use to baptize.

"Yes, but how is it done in your church?" they wanted to know. This direct question deserved a direct answer.

"Well, back home in our church, we follow the method of immersing the person being baptized. However, you do not need to …"

"We'll be baptized by immersion," they stated with finality.

OK, but by whom? Certainly I had no intention of baptizing them. Nor did I think it proper to have anyone from my church background come here to baptize them.

I was functioning as a linguist and translator, not a clergyman. However, I was beginning to realize that although I could not function formally as a clergyman, apart from what they could learn from the scriptures, my wife and I were basically the sole providers of their Christian education. We were the ones who had brought this Gospel message to them, and since they had accepted it, we had a grave responsibility to help them become established in their new faith. So the matter of how they would be baptized was a major problem for us.

Finally we thought of a solution. There were Christians who spoke Balangao, a language spoken over the mountains in Bontoc, a province next to us. They had come to faith in Christ as a result of a New Testament translation there and had already organized into a body of believers. They could not speak Ifugao, but they could speak a trade language, Ilocano, which some Batad people knew. Maybe some of their church leaders would be willing to come here and baptize these babes in Christ. If they would, this would certainly be a testimony of the power of the word to make brothers and sisters out of old enemies.

What a glorious day it was when a small group of Balangao believers arrived in Batad. Although the only language they had in common was Ilocano, it was not more than a few hours before they began using a mixture of Balangao and Ifugao to converse with each other. That Sunday, nine Batad believers were baptized by elders of the Balangao church. This was a time for these nine believers to testify to the Batad people, to people of Balangao, and to the world that they were forsaking the ancestral religion of sacrificing birds and animals to appease spirits and demons. That day the Ifugao Church was formed.

DANCING WITH FIRE

The stillness of a dark Saturday night in Batad was shattered by screaming. We ran to our window and peered out into the blackness. We could see no one and we could not make out a word that was being yelled and there were no close neighbors to inform us. In a few minutes it stopped and we waited for a knock at our door to tell us that someone had been wounded in a fight. Nothing happened. Whatever the disturbance was, we concluded, it did not concern us.

The following morning, we gathered with the Batad believers for a Sunday morning worship service.

"What was the disturbance about last night?" I asked.

"Oh, that was Aginaya," someone responded.

What followed was an amazing story of God's power over demons. Buleng was a new believer. He had been saved from the typical Ifugao background of spirit worship and sacrifice, and was hungry for the word, so he had been reading it constantly. On that dark Saturday night, there was a sacrificial ceremony being conducted under a house next door to his, and he watched the happenings from his house.

When a priest was possessed by a demon, he needed to demonstrate by some supernatural means that he was, indeed, possessed. Ifugao people were as skeptical as we might be about demon possession. It was easy to fake possession unless the possession was verified when the possessed priest could do something that appeared to be supernatural. One way is to grab burning coals in his hands and dance with them without burning his hands. I had witnessed this practice many times. On one occasion after we got to know our neighbors and friends well, I watched this happening and wanted to test for myself what effects this might have on the priest's hands. So as soon as the dancing priest threw down the coals, I took his hands and felt and examined them. They were neither red nor particularly warm. I concluded that this was something not easily explained in the natural realm.

As the ceremony continued next to Buleng's house, Aginaya suddenly caught up flaming embers from a fire and began dancing with them. He circled the courtyard and ended up in front of Buleng. He danced before Buleng with fire coming out through his fingers and waved his hands back and forth to demonstrate his power.

"You see, Buleng," he boasted, "I am —" (He mentioned the demon's name.) "I have power to protect the hands of Aginaya from burning." Buleng was shocked. He had never been challenged by a demon before. What could he respond, now that he was a follower of Jesus Christ?

Then it suddenly came to him—a story from the Bible that he had recently been reading. Standing to face Aginaya, Buleng spoke directly to the demon.

"I have been reading the word of God, and it tells about Jesus relating to his disciples about his death. It said that Peter rebuked Jesus and said, 'Never Lord! This shall never happen to you!' It says that Jesus turned to Peter and, addressing the demon, said, 'Get behind me, Satan!' So I say to you on the authority of God's word: get behind me!"

As he said this, Aginaya lost his power to hold live coals, and his hands were burned. Shamed, he ran from the hamlet out into the night. In keeping with Ifugao custom, he stood on the mountainside facing Batad in the darkness and shouted—for the entire village to hear—curses and threats at Buleng for shaming him in front of the people who had gathered. God was indeed vindicating his children and giving them the power to combat the forces of hell.

TO THE ENDS OF THE EARTH

The Message was being read in the Ifugao language during one of the services of the little Batad church group. This was a common occurrence. In fact, the reading and discussing of a scripture passage was the central part of any service. There were no pastors or even trained church elders yet, so without an ability to read and discuss the relevance of the word to their everyday lives, there would have been no services at all.

On one occasion, the new believers were reading from Acts 1. The story was about the last words of Christ before he went up into heaven. The reader read these words: "You will receive power when the Holy Spirit comes on you; and you will be my witnesses in Jerusalem, and in all Judea and Samaria, and to the ends of the earth." When the phrase "to the ends of the earth" was read, Ilat spoke up with a wide grin on his face.

"That's us!" he exclaimed excitedly. "We live at the end of the earth, and this Message has finally come to us!"

GINID'S LITTLE TABLE

Ginid was a fervent believer. He came to know the Lord early in Batad as the word was taken to the various Batad hamlets. He loved the Lord and his word. The Ifugao style of living was not conducive to being able to sit and enjoy reading and studying the word for extended periods of time. There were no chairs to sit on and no tables to work on, so Ginid solved this problem for himself. He made himself a table. It was no ordinary table. The legs of his table were only a foot long. We visited Ginid one day and observed him at his little table. He sat squarely on the ground with his feet and legs tucked under the table. The scriptures were spread out on the table in front of him, and, with paper and pencil, he was jotting down truths that he was finding in God's word. This was a good example of how dedicated our Ifugao friends were in searching the scriptures.

ILAT, A FAILURE AT INNOVATIVE AGRICULTURE

Ilat struggled to find his place in the developing church and the translation that was making it possible. He was eager to work at the translation desk, yet the farther this work progressed, the more difficult it was for Ilat. It wasn't that he didn't have a clear grasp of his own language or that he could not learn the principles necessary to do a good job helping in the translation project. It was just that in the intense process of untangling difficult passages and examining various ways that a concept might be expressed, Ilat simply became confused and lost. The bewildering demands of groping for new words and ways to express new concepts and the demands for accuracy would send his mind spinning, and he would be unable to give useful responses. The problem was further complicated by the fact that both Bubbud and Bon'og were becoming more and more adept at this task. In the end, Ilat and I both agreed that, since Bubbud and Bon'og were able to take over full translation responsibilities, Ilat could be released to do other things. But what other things?

Besides providing a translation of the New Testament for Ifugao, we were also anxious to encourage the development of small agricultural projects that might improve the standard of living of these people. For centuries they had completely relied on rice, sweet potatoes, yautia, mustard, various crawling things from the fields, and occasionally fish and shells from the pond fields for food. Clothing consisted mainly of what they themselves were able to weave. Developing a cash source, Doreen and I thought, would allow them to break out of this restrictive economic situation.

With this goal in mind, we encouraged Ilat to develop a chicken-raising project. We would provide guidance in how to go about raising chickens. We planned to build chicken cages and bring special chickens from Manila. The chicken feed would come from feed stores just outside of Ifugao. We would also provide the money necessary for him to get started. It seemed to us that this would be a good way for him to continue to live in Ifugao and still be involved in the emerging church. A hotel had just been built in Banaue, and this provided the prospect of a place to sell both broiler chickens and eggs. The hotel was a government project, and we were encouraged by those responsible to develop this project as a chicken and egg source for them.

Chicken raising in Batad, Ifugao

Ilat built cages for his chickens so that they would be confined. Chickens, especially the breed that we brought in, needed to be confined and kept in sanitary conditions. Without it, they would soon become sick and die. The average Ifugao farmer was unaware of the need for a sanitary environment for chickens and livestock. Our advice to Ilat was, for the most part, verbal. We simply did not have time to inspect his project on a daily basis to be sure that he was maintaining sanitary conditions for his chickens. When we did inspect his project, to put it mildly, we found the chickens in an unsatisfactory condition. Constant reminders to Ilat about what he would need to do to maintain a healthy flock did little good, and thus within a few months his chickens became sick and the project collapsed completely. It became obvious that Ilat was not able to function as anything other than a traditional Ifugao farmer. Being from a poor family, Ilat had no means of providing a better life for himself and his family as a traditional farmer. Innovative methods of farming were not something that Ilat could grasp.

ILAT, A SUCCESSFUL COLPORTEUR

Ilat's shoulders drooped as he shuffled into my study, his face downcast.

"Ilat, what is it? What's the matter?" I asked with sudden concern. He was always the carefree one, on top of things, quick with that winning smile—but not today. Something was bothering him.

"I've made my decision," he announced with determination. "I'm going to Manila." We were planning a brief trip to the city from our mountain home as we were finally coming to the end of a first-draft translation of the New Testament into Ilat's language. He could come along.

"What will you do during your visit there?" I tried to keep a growing concern out of my voice, guessing that there was more to his announcement than appeared on the surface.

"I won't be visiting," he replied uneasily, "I'm going there to look for work."

Work? In Manila? Unthinkable!

"But Ilat," I protested, beginning to realize the reason for his discouragement, "what of your work here in the church?" He was a fine witness to the Message, still so new in Ifugao. Ilat had embraced his faith with fervor, and from the beginning had been eager to share it. He was not a dynamic preacher. In fact, he wasn't a preacher at all. He lacked the charisma so often thought necessary for a successful Christian leadership ministry. Nonetheless, through his faithful witness, dozens of villagers had responded to God's message as he met with them one-on-one in their homes, on the trails, or in the rice paddies. With his ever-present smile, he gently and patiently reasoned with them from the Ifugao New Testament books that he always carried with him. I could only imagine the depth of his discouragement. He had been a good language teacher, having worked patiently with me when I was learning Ifugao. As we got into translation, however, he began to realize that he was floundering and had finally quit. He had been no more successful with our farming experience. Undoubtedly, he considered himself a failure.

I continued encouragingly, "Ilat, God is using you here—you know that!"

"Yes," Ilat agreed, "but I have a wife and four little ones to feed and another one on the way! You know my rice fields are just not enough." I understood his plight only too well. Ilat was from a poor family, even by Ifugao standards, and it was a constant struggle to provide even the bare necessities for his family. How could I ask him to stay?

"Well," I responded, not knowing what else to say, "let's ask the Lord about it." So we prayed together, as we had so often done before.

In Manila we went about our business, buying supplies for the next several months, seeing doctors, and checking with our office about various aspects of our work. The second evening, Mary Granaas, our guesthouse hostess, stopped me.

"I see Ilat is in town," she said in a casual voice. The expression on her face betrayed her more than casual interest. She had been to Ifugao and had shared with us the joy of seeing what God was beginning to do. "I thought you had been praying about a Bible distribution ministry. Why isn't Ilat doing that?"

I had talked casually to Mary and others about the possibility of distributing New Testaments to remote locations. As yet, there were no patterns among our colleagues in the Philippines to follow. What would we be getting into?

"Is the problem money to support Ilat and his family?" she asked.

"Well, partly, but …"

"Alright," she said with resolve. "You ask God to guide you in helping Ilat be a missionary to his own people, and I'll ask him to provide the financial means to do it."

So the colportage ministry was born. The colportage was a scripture distribution program in Ifugao that would eventually take the translated word to every corner of that Philippine province and beyond. Upon our return to Batad, Ilat was elated. He vigorously went about the task of packing an old army packsack I had with a change of clothing and a flashlight, filling the rest with New Testament books.

Weeks went by, and finally I began to hear reports of the favorable response to Ilat's labors. One day, a weary hiker, a Christian friend from our village, came by my study on his way home from a long trip. He told a thrilling story of the acceptance of the Message in Patpat, a village not far from us where he had just visited.

When he left, I closed my eyes and prayed, "Thank you, Lord, for allowing Ilat's talents to blossom and bear fruit." I could imagine the scene my friend had just described. A group of women in one of those beautiful terraced rice paddies, harvesting newly ripened grain, singing praises to God, rejoicing in their new-found faith. Indeed they were reaping a rich and joyous harvest, and so was Ilat.

BACK FROM THE JAWS OF DEATH

Ilat's ministry of distributing the word of God to other places almost ended before it began. We attended a Batad church service one Sunday morning, and when the service was finished, Ilat came to us with a worried look on his face.

"Inyap has been bleeding ever since she delivered our baby girl, Ester, a couple of days ago," he explained. "Is there a medicine you can give for that?" Neither Doreen nor I knew much about obstetrics, and I hardly knew how to answer him.

"I know very little about this, Ilat," I responded, "but we'll come over to your house and talk about it. One thing I do know is that Inyap must lie down with her hips elevated and not get up until the bleeding stops."

When we arrived, Inyap was lying on the floor of their tiny house and she did have a pillow under her hips. As we talked about her problem, it became clear that the placenta had not been delivered and that this was the cause of her problem. The nearest medical clinic was in Banaue, fifteen kilometers away. There was no vehicle available to take her there. At the time, I was unaware that this situation had the potential of being very serious for Inyap.

"I do have an injection of vitamin K and this may have some beneficial effect," I suggested. I knew that vitamin K was sometimes used as a coagulant, but I didn't really think that it would be of much use in this situation. "Just stay lying down, and we'll pray that things will be OK for you." Having said that, we prayed and left.

Very early Monday morning, before we were out of bed, we heard frantic footsteps on our back stairs. Our bedroom was next to these steps, so I got up and leaned out the window. It was Ilat. A look of deep distress was on his face.

"Inyap is bleeding again and is much worse!" he wailed.

I hurriedly dressed and followed Ilat to their house. I was utterly shocked. Their house, as all traditional Ifugao houses, was on four foundation posts with the floor elevated about five feet, allowing a space under the house for people to sit and visit or work. Coming down through the floorboards was a stream of blood about the size of my little finger, making a frothy circle below. Even my limited medical experience told me that this was indeed a grave situation. I knew that I was helpless to do anything of a medical nature for Inyap.

"Ilat," I groaned, "there's only one thing we can do now, and that is to get Inyap to Banaue to Dr. Irvine's medical clinic. Make up a hammock and call several strong men and prepare to carry Inyap to Banaue. In the meantime, I will contact a doctor in Manila and see if there is anything I can do here." With that instruction, I quickly left. A hammock required a long bamboo pole onto which would be lashed a strong blanket. The patient would lay inside the blanket, lengthwise to the pole, which was shouldered by a man at each end.

Back at our house, I waited until the Manila radio operator came on the radio net for our morning roll call. Before the roll call began, I related to him what was happening in Batad and asked that he inform Mary Granaas, the Manila guesthouse hostess. I also requested him to arrange for me to talk to a medical doctor by phone patch if this was possible. This he did, but the medical doctor informed me that if I had had no medical training, there was nothing I could do. We would simply have to get the patient to a medical doctor. Of course, he had no idea what this entailed in this faraway place.

Mary Granaas was not only good at her job of managing the guesthouse; she was also a prayer warrior and knew how to intercede for others. She knew Ilat and Inyap and their family well because she had visited us in Batad and because she had been instrumental in allowing Ilat to remain in Ifugao to distribute the New Testament among his people. The Ifugao work had become a special prayer concern for her. She quickly closeted herself in her room and, on her knees, began to pray.

"Oh Lord," she implored, "Ilat and Inyap are your children. Inyap is needed in this life to be Ilat's companion. You have allowed Ilat to embark on a venture of eternal proportions. He is now just beginning to take your word out over the mountains to other valleys to share it with people who have never had it. In order for this to happen, Inyap stays at home and takes care of their four children. She now has a fifth, but she is in great trouble." Mary continued to beseech the Lord. "Please, Lord, give me a sign. Give me a sign that you will touch the body of Inyap and heal her." She was on her knees, and her Bible was open before her.

Then, as though in answer to her prayer, an article she had recently read about the Gospel of Luke flashed into her mind. This article made the statement that Luke had been a physician, and to support this claim it mentioned a number of areas in Luke's writings where he used medical terms. One of these places, according to the article, was in Luke 8, which tells the story of a woman who had been subject to bleeding for a period of twelve years. When she touched the hem of Jesus' garment, according to the King James Version, "immediately her issue of blood stanched." The writer had pointed out that in Greek the word "stanched" was a medical term. Mary flipped open her Bible to that page and read the story. Her eyes came to rest on the words "immediately her issue of blood stanched."

"Thank you, Lord," she said, her heart bubbling over with gratitude. "You have given me the answer I need."

In Batad, I was on our shortwave radio talking about other things when someone came running up onto our veranda with devastating news: "Inyap is dead!"

I could hardly believe it. How could the Lord allow this to happen? Ilat would now be left with four little ones and a baby without a mother to nurture her. And what of his work distributing the scriptures? I informed the radio operator that Inyap had just died and excused myself.

"I need to go now. They are calling me to go to be with Ilat during this sad time." I made my way down the trail to Ilat's house. In Manila, the radio operator gave Mary the tragic news.

"I can't believe this," she responded. "The Lord just told me that Inyap would live!" Immediately she assembled the Filipino house staff, and they bowed again in prayer, imploring the Lord to save Inyap's life.

As I ran along the path to Ilat's house, I passed three women squatting and talking quietly together.

"Is it true that Inyap has died?" I asked them.

"Yes," they replied, "it is true. Inyap is dead."

Farther along, I came upon Duntug, a priest, standing beside the trail and looking out over the valley. He was shouting, "Inyap, Inyap, come back! Don't you pity your newborn baby? Come back! Come back!"

Then it must be that she was indeed dead. I walked into Ilat's yard. First I glanced at the floorboards of his house. No more blood was streaming down, but there was a huge pool of frothy blood to indicate what had happened; Inyap had bled to death. Ilat was sitting with head bowed and with Bon'og and other believers trying to comfort him. The prepared hammock was lying to one side. Ilat's non-Christian relatives and neighbors would have nothing to do with him. His father had urged him to allow sacrificing to be made to the spirit world for Inyap to be cured, and Ilat had refused. So this was the result. He was obviously to blame.

I sat with them, joining my voice with theirs to comfort Ilat as best we could. Then I suddenly had an urge to see Inyap myself. I knew that she was in the little house with a few other women. I excused myself and climbed the ladder. When my eyes adjusted to the darkness inside, I saw four women, one holding Inyap in a semi-sitting position. As I squatted on my haunches, I saw the woman holding Inyap pick up a glass of water to put it to her lips to pour it down her throat. This was customarily done when a person died to moisten the mouth and throat. It was also a cause of drowning some who were at the point of death.

"Stop!" I cried. "Don't do that! Inyap isn't dead!" I could hardly believe my own words. It was as though I was not the one talking. She had all the appearance of being dead, and everyone there assumed that she was. I had, too, except at that moment. I didn't have time for gentler urging. It was a case of life and death. The women were utterly amazed and must have thought that I had lost my senses. However, our reputation of curing the sick was powerful, and so they did as I asked. I checked for vital signs and could find none—no breath, no heartbeat, no signs of life at all. I could find absolutely no sign that Inyap was still alive. Yet I persisted. I backed down the ladder.

"Ilat, your wife isn't dead!" I said with a voice that expressed far more faith than I actually had. "You must get her into this hammock and get her to the doctor in Banaue." With great incredulity, they did as I instructed them. Inyap's list-less body was put into the hammock, and, with one strong man at each end of the pole, they started out.

"Inyap will be in shock," I said. "I'll run home for a blanket and meet you on the trail above." I ran home, quickly got a blanket, and caught up to them on the trail. They paused while I put the blanket around Inyap. It was then that I saw a slight flicker of Inyap's closed eyes. She wasn't dead! However, she would cer-tainly need medical attention, and soon.

It was a five-hour hike to Banaue. Along the way Inyap had moved her body, and the group became aware that although Inyap had not regained consciousness, at least she was alive. The men were tired, but at least they would get medical help here. They carried her straight through town and up the mountainside to the clinic. Incredulous as it was, Dr. Irvine was not there! He had gone on a brief trip to Manila. There was no one at the clinic who could administer transfusions. The result was that Inyap got no medical attention in Banaue at all. We concluded that the Lord wanted to perform a major miracle without man's intervention.

They brought Inyap to Banaue on Monday, and by Saturday she was strong enough to hike over the trail back into Batad. It was a miracle for all to see. God had vindicated Ilat's faith and the faith of Mary and others in Manila. The priests who had criticized Ilat so severely fell silent. This was a great day of vic-tory for the Christian Church in Batad and throughout Ifugao. That Sunday was devoted to thanksgiving for giving Inyap new life, and thus the colporteur ministry continued.

ESTER'S MIRACULOUS RECOVERY

Satan was not finished with Inyap, her daughter Ester—whose birth had almost cost Inyap her life—or with Ilat and the colporteur ministry. It was as though he was determined to turn this great victory into final defeat.

Ester's miraculous recovery from sickness happened years later, in 1980[1], after many life-changing events had happened in Ifugao. Doreen had succumbed to that dreaded disease, leukemia, and was with the Lord. I had brought my new bride, Johanna (Jo), with me to the Philippines. We had left our Ifugao work and

---

1. The story of Ester's Miraculous Recovery is not in chronological order with the rest of the book. It is related here as a continuation of how God provided protection and victory over evil forces attempting to disrupt Ilat's ministry.

were working in Manila. By this time the Lord had given us a daughter, Cheryl, and she was two years old.

Ester, who was nine years old by this time, became extremely sick with both meningitis and encephalitis. Working in Manila, I was not in close contact with what was going on in Ifugao. Ilat had sent me a message by radio that Ester was very sick and he was taking her out of Batad to seek medical help. I was in my office that morning trying to concentrate on my work, but the thought of Ilat and Ester would not leave my mind.

Unknown to me, Ilat had come to Banaue with Ester. Nurses at the Batad clinic had given Ester an intravenous drip, and in order for it to flow, Ilat had to keep the bottle elevated above Ester's head. He persuaded the jeepney he was riding in to take him to the Good News Clinic up a steep hill on the far end of Banaue. When he got there, he discovered that the doctor had gone to Manila. He decided to try to find help at the little Catholic medical clinic on the other end of town, which was about a thousand feet below. So with great difficulty he started out again, carrying Ester with the intravenous drip bottle above her head.

On reaching that clinic he was again completely frustrated. The clinic had no doctor and the nuns were unable to help Ester. The only alternative now was to go to Lagaue, the capital of Ifugao. It was some thirty kilometers away over a very rough road, but there was a provincial hospital there. So he started climbing the mountain into the center of town. Along the way he was overtaken by a jeepney that offered him a ride. It was going to Lagaue, but the fare was more than Ilat had, and he was afraid he would not be able to ride. The driver, however, saw the terrible situation Ester and Ilat were in and agreed to take them to Lagaue without payment of a fare.

In Manila, the burden I felt for Ilat and Ester was more than I could ignore. I had no idea where they were or what had happened to them. By this time we had a helicopter to service translators in the north. I contacted our northern pilot and asked if he would go to Lagaue to see if Ester and Ilat were there. He could undoubtedly find a place to set down. Banaue was completely out of the question. If they were in Lagaue, I asked that he fly them to Manila where they could get adequate medical help.

The pilot agreed and when he reached Lagaue he was amazed that his timing was so accurate; he arrived at the same time that Ilat and Ester did. He flew them to Bagabag and transferred them to a small plane for the trip to Manila. A missionary nurse from South Africa went with them. On the way Ester began to convulse, and once or twice the nurse thought that Ester had died. An hour later they arrived in Manila and arrangements were made for Ester to be admitted to the Polymedic General Hospital.

Ilat and Ester went directly to the hospital, where they were met by James, Ester's brother, who was studying in Manila. We knew that Ester was critically ill. Later that evening, James came to us with a message that Ilat was asking for us at the hospital. Ester was convulsing terribly and was not expected to live. We arrived to find Ilat packing his things to leave. Ester was periodically convulsing.

"I've seen too much of this kind of sickness!" he cried. "I know what's coming. Ester is dying, and I can't stay to watch the horrible thing that is happening to her."

"Ilat," I countered, "don't you remember all the wonderful things that have happened to your family, how the Lord has blessed you and answered so many of your prayers and our prayers in such a miraculous way? Surely he can do it now if we trust him."

Ilat responded in a weak voice, "Go ahead and pray if you still have faith that God can touch my daughter. My faith is exhausted. I can see that she is going to die."

I prayed and pleaded with God to spare the life of this little girl for his glory as he had done for her mother nine years ago. As I prayed, the convulsions seemed to subside. We sat talking of how God had guided and used Ilat in so many ways over the years.

"I really believe that he is going to cure your daughter," I assured him. Finally we left. Ilat decided to unpack his belongings and wait it out.

Ester did live, although she remained in a pitiful condition. The disease and convulsions had left her right hand and foot grotesquely twisted. She was also comatose. When we visited her and Ilat, I was almost sorry that I had prayed that she would live. Her body was hardly alive, and mentally she was a vegetable. As the weeks turned into months, her eyes finally opened in a glassy stare and she could swallow liquids and very soft foods by spoon. There was still no apparent recognition of anything or anyone around her.

The time had come when she must leave the hospital. The attendant doctors assumed that she would remain in a semi-vegetative state for the rest of her life. My faith after these several months had been gradually depleted. It was decided that she would remain in our home in Manila for a few weeks, where she could be brought back to the doctors periodically until they felt it would be safe for her to go back to Ifugao. We prepared a room for her and brought her home. That afternoon, our daughter Cheryl and our little Pekinese dog were playing in Ester's room when Cheryl tripped over the dog. There was a chuckle that came from Ester's lips. She had not only seen what had happened, but it struck her as funny. Jo went in to find Ester responding to things around her, though she still could not talk. Jo called me from my office, and I could hardly believe what was happening. Ester was rapidly improving. By that evening she could say her own name, the names of her father and brother, and could count up to ten in her own language. A major miracle!

However, her right foot was still severely twisted and the tendon at the back of her foot was so taut that the front of her foot was pulled severely downward. She wanted to walk, but with her foot in this condition it was impossible. When she returned to the doctor, he was amazed. He conceded that Ester's rapid recovery was indeed a miracle. However, with her foot in this position, she could not walk. He had seen similar cases, and in order to allow for some sort of mobility, it was necessary for the tendon at the back of the leg to be cut. This surgery would allow the front of her foot to be raised. This would allow her to become barely mobile, though she certainly could not navigate the terrain of Ifugao.

I was resigned to the operation suggested by the doctor, but Ilat would have none of it.

"The Lord has done a miraculous thing in my daughter's body," he pointed out. "I believe he will heal her completely." I thought that Ilat was too unfamiliar with medical matters to realize that this was a permanent condition that Ester would have all her life. The situation was now reversed. I could not talk Ilat into allowing the doctor to schedule an operation. We went home with Ester's foot still crippled.

However, within a day we could see that God was indeed, going to completely heal her. When we returned to the doctor the following week, Ester could almost walk normally. Ilat's faith and God's hand had done what the hand of the physician could not do. Ester went home to Batad healed, able to walk and skip on the terraces and climb mountains like any other normal Ifugao girl. She went on to marry, and she and her husband have two precious children.

Ilat and Ester following Ester's near-fatal sickness

A SECOND VISIT TO PATPAT

After the Lord had snatched Inyap from near death, Ilat was able to continue his colporteur work. We heard glowing reports of what God was doing through him in Patpat and elsewhere. Doreen and I were determined to pay the people of Patpat a visit. Doreen had visited them ten years earlier and was received with detachment and a complete lack of friendliness. We were told that they were responding to the Message and we wanted to witness what changes there might be in their attitude toward people from the outside. With that in mind, we set out early one morning to find out.

The way had certainly not gotten any easier in the past ten years, though we were much more prepared this time for the rigorous hike. Along with several of our neighbors we made our way down to the river, across and up the other side. The two thousand foot climb up the torturous trail helped me better understand the ruggedness of Doreen's historic first trip.

We arrived in Patpat in the cool of midmorning with the satisfaction of successfully reaching our goal. Upon entering a small cluster of houses on the outskirts of the village, we were surprised to see a young boy from Batad, one of our closest neighbors, happily playing with a few boys in the yard of one of the houses.

"What are you doing in Patpat?" we asked. We assumed that he had spent the previous night in Patpat.

"Oh," he responded, "I just came over this morning to play with my friends." He made it sound as though he had just gone next door. This was incredible! We thought we had achieved a major accomplishment, and this little boy "just came over this morning to play"? We decided we probably would not make much mileage here in mentioning the efforts we had exerted in paying a visit to this village.

In the distance, we could hear joyful singing coming from a cluster of houses. As we approached, we were warmly greeted by villagers who were awaiting our arrival. What a happy time it was! There was a time of singing, of exploring the scriptures, of thrilling testimonies of how God had changed and transformed lives. After years of waiting, of preparing seed, it was now beginning to be sown in the hearts of hungry recipients and was springing up to bear abundant fruit.

THE PEOPLE OF PADYAY FIND GOD'S WORD

With Inyap well enough to care for five little ones, Ilat was going farther and farther away from Batad to distribute the scriptures. One day, he reached the village of Padyay, about a seven-hour hike from Batad. Ilat had never been there before, and so he prayed that the Lord would guide him to a house or group of houses where people would be receptive to the Message he was bringing. In one hamlet he found the people curious and friendly, so he stayed with them. As was his Ifugao custom, he did not carry food with him but relied on the people where he went to give him food. When he had had a simple meal, he took out a cassette recorder and began playing hymns that we had prepared for him to carry along with his scripture portions. The people of Padyay had never before seen a cassette recorder, so they began to gather and listen to the singing. They were surprised that it was in Ifugao. They could easily understand it.

Perhaps even more amazing, Ilat had with him some books that he claimed contained the word of God, and when he read from them, the people realized that the books too were in their own language. They could understand what Ilat read! Their curiosity was piqued now, and, before Ilat left to go to another village, they asked him for a copy that they could study themselves. We had completed, in rough draft, the translation of the entire New Testament. As soon as a few books of the New Testament were translated, we had printed them on a mimeograph machine using newsprint paper so that the books would "self destruct" in a few months. We used low quality paper so that when a final version of the New Testament was printed in one volume, people would not be anxious to hold onto the temporary unrevised rough drafts.

By the time we had completed the New Testament translation, there were five volumes in all. The volumes stacked about six inches high. Ilat had three or four copies of these five volumes with him. He gave the people of Padyay a five-book set of the New Testament and left.

Six months went by. Ilat was busy going to other places, so did not have time to go back to Padyay for another visit. During those six months, we found out later, a few of the people of Padyay had learned to read the volumes for them-selves. For six months, night after night, they had gathered together to listen to someone read from these volumes, which Ilat had told them contained the words of God. They were fascinated by the message. Each night, following the reading, they would sit and discuss the relevance to their lives of the message they had heard. They had no missionary to guide them and not even an Ifugao from out-side their village. Obviously the Holy Spirit was there, guiding and directing them to the truths of the scriptures. In the end, they decided that they must seek out this man from Batad and find out more. It was a bold venture. The only other times they had ventured near Batad had been on headhunting raids. They had never before ventured into Batad proper, and they were somewhat fearful. Yet, their desire to know more was strong, so they proceeded.

They arrived in Batad in the late afternoon. They had no idea where they should go, so they entered the first hamlet they came to. It was the hamlet of Babluy, and at that time there were no believers there. They came to the house of the leader in rice agriculture, a prominent local priest.

"We have come to talk to those who are following a new way," they began. "We understand there is an American here also who is translating the message about this into our language."

"Oh," the priest responded, "you do not want to talk to them. There are only five or six who follow that religion. Almost everyone rejects that teaching. It is of no value." The priest offered to give them food and a place to stay that night before returning home the next day. He and one or two others with him were determined not to allow these people to speak to the Christians of Batad.

However, the men of Padyay were determined and were not about to be dis-couraged so easily. They did stay with the priest that night, but early the follow-ing morning they continued their search for believers. They found several believers in the hamlet of Higib who brought them to our house where Bon'og and I were translating.

It was a time of rejoicing. We were spellbound listening to them tell of the hunger of the people of Padyay to become Christians, of their long journey to Batad and how that they had been detained by the priest of Babluy. They wanted to know if we would come to Padyay and give them more instructions about how to become followers of Jesus Christ and how to worship him as a group. Bon'og and a roomful of believers who had gathered at our house agreed that we would do this. We had an impromptu praise service to celebrate this newfound fellowship with traditional enemies. Knowing that they had accomplished their purpose of coming, the five men from Padyay returned home.

It was early on a Saturday morning that we began our trek to Padyay. Six Batad church elders and several other people accompanied me. I had very little understanding of where Padyay was and the kind of terrain we would hike through to get there. Apart from a canteen on my hip and a walking stick, I carried very little with me. Although it was early, the day was already hot. We descended to the Batad River, and then began to climb the eastern mountainside against the dazzle of the rising sun. Once over the crest, we descended into the village of Patpat. It was already midmorning, and we had several hours yet to hike. After a brief rest and visit with Patpat believers, we veered to the left and entered a dense subtropical forest.

Hiking was often treacherous. At one point, we crossed a deep, narrow chasm on nothing more than a huge tree that had been felled to provide a bridge. There were no guardrails and no flat surface to walk on; just the round tree trunk. My supply of water soon ran out, and I became extremely thirsty. I had no idea that it could be so hot at an altitude this high. I was sweating profusely. We rested under a huge tree, and it provided an oasis of shade in the midday glare. While we rested, some of the men scoured the forest for reeds of a particular variety that contained about a teaspoon of water each. About fifty of these reeds were enough to quench my thirst. This was done three times during the course of our hike to Padyay.

We arrived in Padyay in late afternoon. After drinking what seemed to be gallons of water and eating a good meal of rice and a chicken, I was ready to fall asleep. The Padyay villagers, however, had other plans. Just after dark, from all corners of Padyay, we began to see little lights streaming down the mountainsides. They came from all directions, crossed the terraces, and converged on the hamlet where we were resting. *Could we not just meet tomorrow?* I thought to myself. *I am so tired!*

After expressions of welcome and handshakes with at least a hundred people, we began to sing those beautiful hymns that the believers from Padyay had learned from the cassette recorder Ilat left behind on his first visit. Thoughts of sleep or rest quickly vanished. We were caught up in a miracle of what God was doing in Padyay. There was no formal structure to this service, but person after person stood and gave testimony to what God was doing in his or her life. All the strenuous effort exerted during the difficult hike was amply repaid by this one glorious meeting. We eventually got to bed, but it was very late.

Sunday morning dawn broke in a wash of pale yellow behind the dark line of the mountains. It promised to be a good day, a day of worship and rejoicing, of uniting our hearts together here and with other Christians around the world. After waiting so many years, we were finally experiencing the light of the Gospel as it began to break through into the valleys of Ifugao. The morning service was long with the Batad elders leading. There was much scripture reading, and Bon'og gave a challenge from the word suited to new believers.

At the end of the service, Bubbud announced that there would be a baptismal service. He invited any who felt that they were ready to follow Jesus Christ to come forward and be interviewed to see if they were ready for the important step of baptism. They would be examined and baptized by the Batad elders. I wondered if anyone, really, was ready for baptism. They were, after all, very new believers, and they had had no background at all in the Christian faith. I wondered if anyone would know what the significance of baptism was. I knew, though, that it was not my place to decide these matters. I was a foreign observer who had brought the word to them, but the Church in Ifugao was forming without my direct involvement. I was only an observer of what God was doing, and a spiritual consultant when my help was needed and requested.

They came before the Batad elders one by one, two by two, or three by three. Husbands and wives came together; women or men came alone; young people came alone, in pairs, or in groups of three. I listened to their testimonies as they came. Adult men and women gave testimony of years serving the spirit world and of a determination to put that behind them to follow the Lord. Old people determined that now, before they died, they wanted to forsake their old life and put their lives into the hands of the Lord. I was impressed by a couple of young girls, maybe ten or twelve years old, who came and said that they had decided to stop following the demons and wanted to follow Jesus. I was impressed that these young children knew that to follow demons was evil and had made a decision to follow Jesus instead. Though these people obviously did not know much about the intricacies of Christian theology, they certainly knew what they were doing.

We made our way down to where a small stream pooled, creating a body of water large enough to be used as a place for them to be baptized. It was a beautiful sight. The terraces around us were lush green with growing rice, and the banyan trees, reflected in the still water, provided us with refreshing shade from a blazing noontime sun.

I stood watching as each of the seventy people was baptized. *It is true*, I thought, *that the Ifugao rice terraces are an Eighth Wonder of the World.* Yet, a greater wonder was the sight of these precious children of God showing their neighbors and the world that they were determined to follow the one who had created all this natural beauty and had also created these, his beautiful children. Seventy people were baptized that day, and the church of Padyay was born!

BANTER AND EVANGELISM

The verbal contest of banter—a common Ifugao cultural feature—can be used not only for the purposes of relaxation and fun but more seriously to establish the credibility of a participant's point of view or to convince someone of a particular truth. Ilat was beginning to use this technique to spread the Message of the Messiah. He had become quite proficient in his ability to use the word of God to convince his friends of the claims of Christ on their lives. Meeting someone along a trail, he would squat on his haunches, requiring the other person, following Ifugao culture, to do the same. Betel nut chew would be exchanged in a gesture of friendship, and a lively conversation would ensue. Steering the exchange to spiritual subjects, Ilat would skillfully use the word to engage his friend in a bantering contest. He rarely lost, and commonly it ended with the friend realizing that he or she was, in fact, arguing not with Ilat but with God. Scores of people of the area came to knowledge of Christ and of the New Way through this procedure.

On one occasion, Ilat and two other Batad men were in Hinalong, some two days' hike from home. It was their first visit, and people were curious to hear what this book that he had brought had to say. Among them was a leader named Ngippul. He had never heard a message like this before, and he was skeptical. He had very many questions to ask. Finally he spoke to Ilat.

"Come to my house, and let's discuss this matter in private. I have many questions that need answers." So Ilat left his two friends behind with the group and went off with Ngippul to his house. Almost immediately a bantering contest began, but with a difference. This one was in dead earnest! For each question raised by Ngippul, Ilat would flip through the pages of his book and read an answer. This went on for some time until, with not a little exasperation, Ngippul vented his frustration.

"Ilat, just lay that book aside, and let's talk man to man."

"If I were to lay the book aside," Ilat responded, "I would have nothing to say. Your argument is not with me but with God."

So the questions resumed with answers from God's word. Discussion continued well into the night. Finally, Ngippul fell silent.

"What other questions do you have?" Ilat wanted to know.

"I have none," Ngippul responded. "I am convinced that this Message is true. I want to be a follower of Jesus Christ." In this simple way, Ngippul's life was transformed. Ngippul continued, "My wife is inside our house sleeping. I must wake her and tell her, too, of this New Way!" Roused from sleep and hearing the Message from her own husband, Rosa gave her heart to the Lord.

So, in this way, the Gospel came to Hinalong. In the space of a few weeks a little band of believers was formed in Hinalong with Ngippul as their spiritual leader.

WASHING THE MESSENGERS' FEET

There were times when those carrying the word to distant places were gone for several weeks at a time. When those with families in Batad returned home, we would often spend time praying together and searching the scriptures for answers to the innumerable questions being asked them about this New Way. They would list scores of passages on paper and would eventually commit them to memory as they sharpened their ability to use the "Sword of the Spirit which is the Word of God" (Ephesians 6:18b).

During these times, we listened to their stories of failures and successes, frustrations and joys, fears and bravery. They told of times when the people of inhospitable villages would offer them no food or lodging. They would then be forced to sleep in forests and forage for whatever food they could find—usually roots or tough, bitter berries and fruits. They were often stopped on the trail by revolutionaries who would detain them, question their motives for enduring such hardships, and search their backpacks for antirevolutionary literature. The revolutionaries were puzzled to find only clothing, scripture books, and nothing else. There were also times when people with open arms would welcome them into their homes and give them the best of their meager fare as they listened to the Gospel message of Jesus for the first time.

The colporteurs did not carry spears on their trips to distant places, but they did carry knives, which they commonly carried on their belts. Ilat told us that he had finally come to feel that this practice was wrong. He realized that his life and the lives of the other men were in the hands of the Lord. He felt that he needed to completely put his trust in the Lord for his safety, so he discontinued carrying his knife when he went out.

Debriefing when the colporteurs returned from trips to far places not only provided opportunities for us to learn what was happening in other parts of Ifugao but as we listened we were able to minister to the physical needs of these faithful men. They were not well equipped with proper gear for the rigors of traveling from village to village in rugged regions. Hiking barefoot through rough mountain terrain was especially difficult. On one occasion, as Ilat sat on the porch of our house telling us of his exploits during the past several weeks, he was obviously weary, and his feet were bruised and bleeding. As we had so often done before, with a basin of warm water I washed his feet and applied ointment and bandages. This was a vivid reminder to me of the scripture passage, Isaiah 52:7: "How beautiful … are the feet of those who bring good news."

DANG'UL'S CONVERSION

Dang'ul was a traditional Ifugao priest who lived in a hamlet just below our house. He earned a comfortable living for himself and his family by going house to house and joining in the sacrifice of chickens and pigs to ancestral spirits and demons. He had not responded to the Gospel message and showed no signs of interest in anything but the native religion, which seemed to completely occupy his interest and time.

We had just finished translating Second Corinthians in first draft and were anxious to know how it might communicate. I asked Bubbud and Bon'og to call two or three men to our study to sit with us for a week or so to go through Second Corinthians and see how well they could understand what was written. This was known as a "naïve check" of the book. Dang'ul was one of the men they called. His interest was not to find out what was in the scriptures but to get a little money from the stipend he would receive.

Our procedure was to first discuss the general theme and purpose of the book so that those who had never heard it before would be able to get some idea of what the book was all about. We then would read laboriously through the book section by section, paragraph by paragraph, and finally sentence by sentence. We asked questions that would give us some indication of whether or not the men could understand what the passage was saying. We also discussed what was being taught in each passage.

As the second day of our session came to a close, Bon'og spoke to me privately.

"Did you notice the effect this book seems to be having on Dang'ul?" he asked. "He seems to be thinking deeply about what he is hearing." I had, in fact, noticed that it was having an effect on him. The next day, when Dang'ul left the study to go home, we noticed again that he was deep in thought.

Near the end of the fifth day, it was obvious that Dang'ul was under great conviction. We stopped to rest for a few minutes, and Dang'ul spoke up.

"This book is affecting me greatly," he said with a sigh. "You say that this is the word of God, and I believe it is. And if this is so, then what I am doing as a priest is very wrong. I am ready now to give up my past life and accept Jesus as my Lord and Savior." Then and there Dang'ul became a believer.

By rejecting his past to follow the Lord, Dang'ul was also turning his back on his means of livelihood. Without his activities as a priest, he had little chance of providing an adequate livelihood for his family. He knew it, and we knew it.

Later, Ilat came to me.

"The work of tending to the needs of new groups of believers and at the same time reaching out into new territories is too much for two of us," he pointed out. "Would it be possible for Dang'ul to join our team?"

I knew that financially we were pressed to the limit with just two men serving as colporteurs and evangelists. Could we become braver in trusting the Lord for our financial needs?

"You talk to him," I suggested. "Explain to him the difficulties and dangers and the financial uncertainties. If he is willing to join you and work with a very small and uncertain stipend, then go ahead and include him on your team. Be sure, though, to give him proper training." So Dang'ul became the third member of our colporteur team.

The testimony of Dang'ul, a converted Ifugao priest, provided a compelling witness to older people, especially to other priests.

BENWAG THE PRIEST AND EVANGELISM AT MALOY

One unfortunate development connected with the Christian movement in Ifugao is the fact that, because it is solidly based on the scriptures, those with little or no formal education find it difficult to take leadership roles in witness and worship. This, for the most part, is because older, uneducated people can neither read nor write. While young people have enthusiastically taken a leadership role in the developing church, older people have, for the most part, been sidelined. The result has been a major shift in cultural values from that based on tradition, administered by the elders, to one based on the technologies of the twentieth century, administered by the youth.

Perhaps the situation would be better described as a split. The Ifugao people are tied to a culture of terrace agriculture that, by the very nature of where they live, cannot change. In this respect, they are solidly rooted in traditional agricultural methods without the possibility of mechanized farming. With a few exceptions, this also dictates the kind of food they eat and the kind of houses they live in. However, in terms of religion, there has been a complete turnaround—a revolution. No longer does a majority of them sacrifice or pray to ancestral spirits or demons. Now, the majority worships and prays to God, who created the universe and everything in it. Thus, in the area of religion, for at least one generation, young people dominate and control.

The switch of roles did not deter Benwag from taking a major part in what was happening. He was an old man and an Ifugao priest. He had spent his whole life promoting and participating in the native religion. But all that changed when Ilat and friends brought the Gospel to Benwag's village of Maloy. Benwag listened to the Message as it was read. He knew in his heart that this was indeed the truth, and he simply accepted it without question.

Benwag, although an old man, was still active in the religious world of Ifugao. He made his living by going from hamlet to hamlet, chanting his prayers, and sacrificing chickens and pigs. When he decided to accept Jesus as his Lord and Savior, he was without work. He was fascinated by our machines that could talk. This impressed him with the possibility that, although he could not read, and although he had had no formal schooling, yet he could play a cassette player. So he went to Ilat with a request.

"Do you have one of those machines that I could use?" he inquired. "I have gone from place to place here in Maloy and beyond, praying and sacrificing chickens and pigs to the ancestral dead and to demons. I can't read, but I would like to go back to all those places now and let them listen to the word of God from a cassette player. I want to tell people what has happened in my life." So the old man, Benwag, without any salary or stipend became an evangelist to his own people.

MENITA, A MOST UNLIKELY MISSIONARY

At the other extreme, a young person, Menita, had come to work in our home soon after we entered Ifugao. She wanted to attend school in Banaue, and during our first few years in Ifugao, we lived close enough for her to do so. She lived with us and went to school, working in our home when she had time. We had daily devotions after the evening meal in our home, and Menita was included in these times of reading and memorizing scripture and singing Gospel songs and choruses. Eventually she gave her life to the Lord.

She did not seem to us to have exceptional ability or drive in any area, so we expected that she would settle down, marry one of the young men of the little Christian group that had formed while we lived there, and live for the Lord in that community.

However, the Lord had his hand on Menita in a way that we could not have possibly predicted or even imagined. We returned to America, where I enrolled in graduate school, and when we returned to the Philippines for our second time, we transferred to Batad. We lost track of Menita for a few years, but during that time God was working in her life. For reasons we will not understand until we find out in glory, Menita had a strong burden to take the Gospel to the people of Hungduan, the area where General Yamashita surrendered to Douglas MacArthur during the Second World War. Following the war, this had been a stronghold of insurgents seeking to overthrow the Philippine government.

Menita had several problems to overcome—she was young, she was a girl, and she had had no training to be a missionary to her own people. Yet, Menita had a strong desire to be a missionary, and she eventually persuaded her younger brother to go with her. With nothing more than a handbag carrying her Bible translated in the trade language of Ilocano, a few clothes, and the company of her brother, she began her missionary journey to Hungduan. She was there several months, and during that time, the Hungduan church was formed to the glory of God.

We did not hear about this happening until some time later when we learned that she was sick in the Banaue hospital. We went there to find her so weak that she could hardly talk. She was dying of leukemia. She was able to tell us enough for us to know that before she became sick, God had used her in a wonderful way among the Hungduan people. She died soon after our visit and was buried in her home village in Gohang. We know that the day will come when we will get the full story of how God used this young woman for his glory in a very remote place.

INDALHIN'S VICTORY IN DEATH

It was a special delight for us to witness older people coming to know the Lord. This was because, compared to younger people, making this all-important step of obedience seemed to require greater faith. It was hard for us to imagine the tenacious grip the enemy had on the hearts and lives of someone who had spent a lifetime serving him.

It seemed that this was Indalhin's situation. Her whole life had been spent in the Batad Valley. She had never been to any other place to experience what the rest of the world was like. She spoke only one language, Ifugao, and she knew nothing of any other religion or way of life but her own. She had grown up, married, had children and grandchildren, and now she was nearing the end of her life.

Some of the younger people came to Indalhin with the Message of Jesus. She told them that she was unhappy and dissatisfied with the life she had lived. She longed for something more to fulfill her existence, but she had no idea what that might be. But when they read the Gospel message to her, she seemed to know immediately that that was what she had been longing for. She accepted the Message gladly and became a believer in Jesus. It was nothing short of a personal, life-changing revolution. At the time of her conversion, the little group of believers had multiplied, and she found not only young people but older people as well, with whom she could share her newfound faith.

Eventually, Indalhin fell ill. It was amazing to contrast the way she accepted her illness and the prospect of dying with that of unbelievers without Christ, who were filled with fear and apprehension. This was a crucial test point in her life. She was severely tempted.

"Indalhin," her relatives warned, "you are dying. You know that the demons will be coming to take you to the world of the dead. You must sacrifice to them as you have been taught to do all your life in order to escape their wrath. If you do not, your spirit will be torn to shreds."

"No," Indalhin answered confidently. "I've put my trust now in Jesus Christ. I no longer need to have the priests sacrifice and pray for my soul. It is in the hands of Jesus and he will take care of me in the next life."

Her relatives would not give up.

"If you do not allow the priests to sacrifice and pray, the demons will not only deal harshly with you, but they'll be furious with us, too." Despite their persistence, the peace of Christ ruled in the heart of Indalhin, and she refused to listen.

"If you will trust your lives to Jesus, he will protect you just as he protects me," Indalhin assured them. With this, they left Indalhin and would have nothing more to do with her. She had lost her earthly family.

However, Indalhin still had a family, one based on her newfound faith, God's family. This family rallied around her. They took up the responsibilities that her earthly family refused to perform. They fed Indalhin, bathed and clothed her and set up a twenty-four hour watch around her. Indalhin died with the joy of the Lord on her face and in her heart. She belonged to him and she had gone home to be with her Lord. The Batad believers prepared Indalhin's body for burial. It was propped up under her house, and believers came to pay her their final respects. During this time, songs of praise to the Lord were sung, scripture was read, and prayers of praise were offered to the Lord for preserving the steadfast faith of this dear old saint to the end of her life. We joined them as they took Indalhin's body down over the terrace dikes to a tomb prepared especially for her.

There, again, with singing, praying, and scripture reading, they buried Indalhin, one of the first of the believers to have entered the eternal presence of the Lord she loved and served.

THE CRY OF AN ILLITERATE

Doreen spent much of her time typing up my manuscripts and trying to keep me as much in order as was possible. My work habits involved working on several tasks at the same time, and I found it easiest to have them all before me on my desk. Occasionally, Doreen could no longer tolerate the clutter and would sweep my desk clean and file everything under appropriate subjects. It would take me a week after this to find what I wanted and get back to "normal."

In spite of trying to keep me organized and supervising the work of Lab'an, who worked in our home, she still found time to work on designing and working up primer and reading materials to teach adults to read and to write. One formidable task that she took on was to teach our father, Mannung, how to form the various letters of the Ifugao alphabet, write his name, and begin the process of being able to write down ideas that, until then, he had only expressed orally.

The task seemed to be impossible. Mannung had never attended school, and, as far as we knew, had never held a pencil in his hand. Doreen began by getting him to simply make circles on the page. That seemed to her to be a simple task, but it turned out to be almost impossible for Mannung to accomplish. He would begin to draw, and immediately the line would wander off in a direction that would never make a circle no matter how large the sheet of paper. He was simply incapable of making a circle. So Doreen would take Mannung's hand and guide him. However, he was unconsciously resistant to following her guidance. This wasn't because he didn't want to draw a circle. He was simply incapable of doing it. After months of starts and stops, Mannung finally did learn how to write his own name in at least semi-legible fashion.

After several months, Doreen had an impressive array of primers and reading materials and had taught several classes of Batad adults the art of reading their own language. The promise of using these materials in other areas of Ifugao was hopeful. To do this would require funding an extensive literacy program with missionaries devoted to literacy work. Unfortunately, this never happened. The salvation of the work of evangelism in Ifugao was the fact that the American government first, followed by the Philippine government, had established public schools through grade six throughout Ifugao. Although children were taught to read only English at first, and then English and Filipino in later years, this did have one major advantage. The public schools taught children the English and Filipino alphabets. We had been careful to develop a writing system based on the Roman script. It was necessary to redefine the pronunciation of some sounds, but even so, if they knew the Roman script through learning to read English and Filipino, it was usually a minor jump for them to use that knowledge in developing an ability to read Ifugao.

One young man, Ballug, who later became a colporteur and evangelist, came to our house one day from Patpat. He had accepted Jesus as his Lord and Savior about a week earlier and proudly held in his hand a copy of one of the volumes of New Testament book compilations that we had prepared for use until the entire New Testament was published in a single volume. He sat and read fluently from it with impeccable Patpat Ifugao pronunciation. We were astounded, since no one had taught him to read Ifugao. This certainly boosted our confidence to know that those who had learned the Roman alphabet would be able to teach themselves how to read the Ifugao scriptures.

During a trek through northeastern Ifugao, on one occasion, we were visiting the people of Padyay. As we sat under a house at night in the darkness with a hundred or so people gathered, they shared with us problems that they were encountering in their walk with the Lord. They asked for our suggestions about how they might cope with them. The subject eventually drifted to a discussion about how the zeal and enthusiasm of some believers had declined. One lady, whose face I could not see, spoke up.

"I can tell you why we aren't as enthusiastic now about our faith as we were at first," she suggested. "It is because we can't read God's word for ourselves. We do not know how to read, so we must rely on our children to read to us. We need to be able to use God's word for daily instruction in living our spiritual lives, and we can't do that."

We desperately wanted to be able to say, "We'll teach you," or, "We'll organize a literacy program for you." However, we could not. The geographic area was vast, and the number of people involved was so large! We had another full-time task to accomplish, and that was to continue translating the New Testament scriptures until they were finished. Our hope was that Ifugao people themselves would take up the challenge of promoting and teaching literacy among those who were unable to read.

DOREEN WITH THE LORD

We had spent five years in Batad during our third period in the Philippines. It was now 1971 and time to return home once again. The Lord's hand had rested on Doreen, and during the six years that had gone by since the first signs of leukemia, the disease was in remission and had not returned. During the last six months of our Batad stay, however, there were troubling signs that the leukemia might be lurking somewhere in her body, even though blood tests did not indicate it. She was becoming progressively weak. At night, sometimes, it seemed that unseen forces were bothering her. Only prayer seemed to relieve her fears of the unknown. Hiking out over the mountain was becoming more and more difficult, until, near the end, it was necessary for me to take off my belt, attach it to her waist, and use it to literally pull her up the mountain to the pass above.

We still had hopes that the leukemia was gone and that this was just some temporary physical problem. With that in mind, I had applied once again for a doctoral program at Yale and was again accepted. It was June when we left the Philippines, and by September Doreen found it difficult to walk. The leukemia that had not reared its ugly head for over six years was now back. By the time classes began, it was obvious that I could not both look after Doreen in the condition she was in and simultaneously carry the load of a Ph.D. program. So, for the second time, I declined to enter the program.

Thankfully, we were in New Haven and had no other responsibilities for the winter. So Yale University graciously appointed me as a visiting fellow, which allowed me to audit whatever classes I could. I was given full use of their library, which held over three million volumes. Under the very difficult circumstances we found ourselves in, this was a tremendous opportunity for me to catch up on what had been going on in the academic world since I had been gone those past five years. In the spring, we returned to Edmonton and then later moved to Calgary. The leukemia was now in an advanced stage, and the doctors cautioned me that Doreen would not live much longer. She was completely confined to bed. She was becoming too weak to feed herself.

One day, Doreen suggested that we have the elders of our church pray for her again. *Maybe*, she thought, *the Lord would perform another miracle.*

I arranged for a meeting around Doreen's bedside, and again she was prayed over and anointed with oil. I could hardly believe the result of that time with the elders. The following morning, Doreen was out of bed and making breakfast. Was the Lord going to allow her to live after all? However, it was not to be. In a few days, she was back to her previous condition.

We decided that the Lord was saying to us, "I am with you. I honor your prayers and the prayers of the church elders, but it is now time for Doreen to be with me." Within a few weeks, Doreen was with the Lord to receive her reward for a faithful life spent serving him. On her bronze grave marker are the words: "She gave her life to give the word of God to the Ifugao people of the Philippines."

For the past several years, the possibility of Doreen's being taken from me had always been there. That possibility had been suppressed deep down in my thoughts. In the months that her illness slowly weakened her body, I knew that without the Lord's direct intervention, her death was imminent. Still I was not prepared when it came. I was devastated. I was angry at the Devil for creating a world of sickness and death, and I was extremely lonely. The thought of returning to the Philippines alone was completely incomprehensible to me. Maybe, I thought, my time was over in the Philippines. Yet, try as I might, I could not bring myself to believe that that was what the Lord had planned for me.

I would have a good opportunity to test going back to Batad alone. I had been revising the Ifugao translation in Canada, and, although I could not leave now, I could arrange to go back for three months or so to do some on-site testing. When I arrived, my Ifugao family sensed my loneliness, and they were determined that I would not be alone. After my day's work was finished and Bon'og and our faithful house helper, Lab'an, had gone home, the children of the village descended on me. They were everywhere—in the little living area, in the kitchen, and even in the bedroom. I began reading to them, in Ifugao, the Bible storybooks that Doreen had prepared by pasting Ifugao over English. They loved them. They were on the floor in front of me, at my sides, on the arms and back of my chair, and even a couple on my lap. Except for the fact that most of them had not bathed in days, if not weeks, it would have been enjoyable to have them so unafraid, treating me like a favorite grandfather. When I went to bed, I was able to close my bedroom door, but there they were, sleeping on the bare wood floor just outside. Certainly I was not alone.

THE BUNHIAN CLINIC

It was near the time for me to return to Canada. I was close to being finished with the work that brought me back. While we had been away, the colporteurs, who were now fanning out throughout Ifugao, reported groups of believers in many places. Ralph and Shirley Zielsdorf, a Canadian couple, close friends of Doreen and me, wanted to see what we were reporting of what God was doing in Ifugao.

I decided that a visit to Bunhian—one of the places where there was a positive response to the Gospel—would be a good place to visit. By taking a bus to Mayaoyao and hiking several hours, we could probably reach Bunhian in one day.

The trip to Mayaoyao was uneventful but scary. Our bus was heavily overloaded with a top load of cargo and people that caused the bus to sway dangerously from side to side. It was especially nerve-wracking navigating tight corners. Struggling up steep inclines and maneuvering downhill was equally unnerving. We were packed inside, with no chance of getting out if some problem arose. For most of the way, it was a single-lane roadway, and I wondered what would happen if we met a vehicle going the other way. Fortunately, this didn't happen.

After our three-hour bus ride, we still had to hike five more hours to Bunhian. Along the way, the colporteurs told of some of the difficulties they had encountered hiking on that trail. Several times they had been met by anti-government people who had thoroughly inspected their baggage. They were mystified at why the colporteurs would be carrying stacks of books. These inspections gave the colporteurs an opportunity to tell them about the Message contained in their books.

We arrived in late afternoon, and the people gathered for an evening of singing, Bible reading, and fellowship. They told us that since they had stopped offering pigs and chickens to demons to cure sickness, they felt that there must be a substitute for that, and so they had prayed about the possibility of a medical clinic for Bunhian. They were sure the Lord would answer their prayers, and, in fact, had already picked out a piece of land where they could build a clinic. We agreed with them that a clinic would be a real benefit to them and agreed that we would join them in prayer. I must admit, though, that I had little faith that it could ever become a reality in such an isolated area. I mentioned that in order to have a clinic, an airstrip would be absolutely necessary in order to supply it with medicines and equipment. With that, we continued to sing and worship the Lord late into the night.

The next morning, they wanted to show us the place where the clinic would be built. They had no notion of giving up on the possibility of a clinic. Almost to humor them, we followed them to a grassy area with a small stream running through it. I agreed that this would indeed make an ideal place for a clinic. Ralph, Shirley, and I left the following day, and again I promised them that I, with my friends back home, would pray with them about the possibility of a clinic. Ralph and Shirley went back to Canada, and I went back to Batad to continue my work.

A couple of weeks later, I was driven to our translation center in Bagabag by one of our members who worked there. I would have a final check of the Ifugao translation. I had about three more weeks of work left, and then I would return to Canada.

Along the way, the driver casually mentioned that a doctor, Dr. Eli Sarmiento, was in Bagabag. He worked with his wife, Alma—also a medical doctor—at the Polymedic General Hospital in Manila. He was making plans to begin a Filipino missionary medical program in remote rural areas and was in the north to see if there might be a place there where they could begin their program. This sounded very interesting to me, because I had just been with the group in Bunhian who wanted a medical clinic. I dismissed it as an impossible location, because they lived in an area with no roads and no nearby airstrip where even a small plane could bring in supplies.

I decided that I would at least talk to Dr. Sarmiento about the great desire of these new Ifugao believers. Dr. Sarmiento was highly interested. When I pointed out that there was no place for even a helicopter—let alone a plane—to land, he suggested that we talk to the pilot based at the Bagabag center. The pilot thought that an airstrip could be built there, but in such an area it would involve a major effort, and he, alone in the flying program in the north, was extremely busy. He didn't know when he could get around to actually going into Bunhian to see where an airstrip might be built.

By this time my interest was piqued, and I hoped that I might still be in the area when the Lord began his work. I knew that I was likely to be back in Canada long before the construction of an airstrip could get underway, if, in fact, there could be one. I decided that I would not pressure the pilot by telling him of my tight schedule. If the Lord wanted an airstrip in Bunhian for a medical clinic, then he would have to arrange the details.

Besides no airstrip, there was another problem—Dr. Sarmiento had no finances for his dream! So it was just a dream. Well, of course God could take care of that, too, but this was now becoming quite complicated. I was beginning to think that eventually the people of Bunhian might get their clinic, but it would undoubtedly be a long way off. With that, I said good-bye to Dr. Sarmiento, who was returning to Manila, and I went back to my final check of the translation before leaving Ifugao for Canada.

The next morning, I got a message from the radio operator at the center. Dr. Sarmiento, in Manila, had set up a scheduled time to talk to me. I thought he might have something else that he had forgotten to tell me the previous day. When he began talking, he was so excited that I could hardly understand him.

"You can't imagine what has happened here!" he exclaimed, his words tumbling out in rapid succession.

He told me that an American couple, Mr. and Mrs. Hilgendorf, had recently come to Manila and that Mr. Hilgendorf had gone off to India on a business trip. While he was there he had contracted dengue fever and had come home seriously ill. Dr. Sarmiento's wife, also a doctor, had been assigned to care for him. Tragically, Mr. Hilgendorf had died, and Mrs. Hilgendorf was left with no close friends in a strange country. Dr. Sarmiento asked her to come and stay at their home for a few days while she grieved and planned what she would do next.

During the evening meal, Dr. Sarmiento enthusiastically related what had happened in the north. He explained that the people of Bunhian had given up sacrifice to demons to cure sickness and had accepted the Gospel message. They were extremely anxious for a medical clinic to fill this void.

"We now must try to find financing for the clinic," he said. "It will be expensive, because much of the supplies will have to be flown in by plane or helicopter."

Mrs. Hilgendorf listened intently. When Dr. Sarmiento finished, she said in a quiet voice, "Do you think if I provide the finances for that clinic, it would be a fitting memorial to my husband?" It would indeed! So plans for the Hilgendorf Medical Clinic were begun.

One problem remained, and that was an airstrip. I could see by this time that the Lord indeed was directing this project, but I still felt that the Lord must put it on the heart of the pilot to provide enough time to investigate an airstrip. Two more miracles were to occur to make this happen.

In what seemed a completely unrelated event, the pilot's wife needed to go to Manila for a few days. While there, she and a couple of her friends decided to attend a particular church. She had no way of knowing what would happen during that service. So she was completely surprised when Dr. Eli Sarmiento spoke that morning about plans for a missionary medical clinic in Bunhian.

"We plan to begin work on constructing the clinic," he explained, "as soon as the pilot in the north can go to Bunhian overland and approve a place for constructing an airstrip for the clinic." She had not heard of this project or of any promise by the pilot to go to Bunhian. She almost fell off of her seat. Was there really to be an airstrip in this remote location? Did her husband really say he would go there and scout one out?

She confronted her husband when she got home. Yes, indeed, he had given his assurance that he would do this, but he was extremely busy. It would have to wait. However, just to get some idea of what the land looked like in the area, and because he was flying near Bunhian anyway, he decided to do a flyover to see what he could. He could hardly believe what he saw. There on a mountainside there must have been a hundred people crawling over the land like ants, trying to flatten out an airstrip. He wanted to shout, "Stop! Stop!" But of course no one could hear. Yet they could not just go on digging there. It was completely unsuitable. He made two or three more passes of the area and decided where he would look on the ground.

Two days later he was in Bunhian to stop them from what they were doing. With the help of these eager people he did find another spot that would, with considerable work, be adequate for an airstrip. In less than two weeks, his little plane touched down on the Bunhian airstrip. He was able to give instructions for further improvement and flew off to give us the wonderful news.

The time was drawing near for my return to Canada, but the last thing I did before I left was fly into Bunhian with Dr. Sarmiento and Mrs. Hilgendorf for the dedication of the airstrip.

It was an occasion of great rejoicing. The mayor of Mayaoyao came for the dedication, as did hundreds of people from the area. It was a testimony to the faithfulness of our Lord, who had blessed and honored the faith of a people who were just beginning to trust him. So the people of Bunhian and surrounding areas had no further need to sacrifice to demons for the cure of their sicknesses. As they turned to the Lord, they now had a clinic, the Hilgendorf Medical Clinic.

OUR RETURN

Back in Canada, I could complete my preparation of the Ifugao New Testament for publication. I had been in Canada for five years, and I longed to get back to my second home among the people I loved. It had been a year and a half since Doreen had gone to be with the Lord, and I was still alone and very lonely.

Johanna Schipper had been my secretary in Canada for two years. She was a single young lady, and I had disrupted her plans to go to Surinam by asking her to work temporarily as my secretary. We had worked very well together, and she was a very compatible person to work with. Johanna—or Jo, as she is known to close friends—was over twenty years younger than me, and although I had had fleeting thoughts of her becoming my life partner, I hadn't really thought that it would happen. At this stage in my life, I wasn't really into dating women, let alone younger women. I was still grieving the tragic loss of my precious wife.

Nevertheless, one day I asked Jo out on a date. She readily accepted. I was now finishing my work in Canada and would leave soon for the Philippines. Our courtship lasted a month and, with minor hesitation at first, Jo accepted my proposal to become my life partner. The joy that she brought into my life was the first time that I had really experienced joy since Doreen's death. I was reminded of the verse, "... weeping may remain for a night, but rejoicing comes in the morning" (Psalms 30:5b). This verse expressed very vividly what I was experiencing. A few weeks later, in early 1977, Jo and I traveled back to the Philippines.

7

WORD POWER

AN IFUGAO WAR DANCE

The day finally arrived in June, 1977, for the dedication and distribution of the New Testament in a single volume. All the years we had worked on this project with the joys and sorrows that accompanied our work had finally come to an end, and the Ifugao people were getting at least this portion of God's word. Elaborate preparations were made, and we were involved in arranging the main service. Doreen had had a major part of all of this, and we hoped that somehow she was with us to observe this glorious event.

Following the main service and distribution of a few gift volumes for those who were involved in its translation, a time for selling New Testaments followed, and many people bought copies at a fraction of what it had cost to produce them. This was followed by a feast of boiled pigs, rice, and vegetables.

The Ifugao Christians wanted to have an evening event, so we left it to them to decide and direct the evening's activities. It was an evening of thanksgiving to God for placing in our hearts the need to leave our home in Canada to come here and translate his word into Ifugao. The evening was also a testimony to what the word had done in individual hearts and to the tribal group in general.

While this was all going on, there was a startling whoop and cry as several Ifugao warriors—holding shields and spears, and dressed in their full regalia of colorful loincloths, with bolos strapped to their waists with seashell-decorated belts—rushed in from the darkness. To the beat of throbbing brass gongs they danced around in a circle. At the end, they threw down their shields, spears, and bolos in a heap on the ground. One of them, in typical Ifugao fashion, stood with spread legs and shouted for all to hear.

"We are Ifugao! For centuries past we have been a warlike people. We have killed our enemies, we have taken their heads, and we have offered them to demons. But today the word of God has come to us. We have heard it because it is in our own language and we have accepted it. We throw down our implements of warfare to show that we are finished with our old life of hatred and killing and we accept the new life in Jesus Christ."

A TREK THROUGH IFUGAO

I had been gone five years. During that time, I had lost my loving partner who had so faithfully worked with me to provide the translated word for the Ifugao people. God had been gracious to me in providing another loving partner. We had come back and we had brought the New Testament with us, which was being distributed throughout this rugged countryside. During the time I had been away, the men who distributed the word in those temporary five volumes had been reporting success after success as people embraced the Message in the farthest corners of Ifugao. When Doreen and I left, three church groups had formed—one in Batad, one in Patpat, and one in Padyay. They now told me that there were thirty-five church groups. I wanted to visit as many as I could, and I wanted to introduce them to Jo, my new bride. We planned a three-week hike of Ifugao, beginning in Batad, going through Mayaoyao and Bunhian, and ending in Potia on the eastern border of Ifugao.

The country we would hike through would be extremely rugged, so I encouraged Jo to hike with me in very difficult areas in and around Batad. She could not believe that we would be experiencing places as difficult as some of the sharp mountain edges we were practicing on, but I assured her that they would not only be equally as difficult but in some cases more difficult.

After practicing for a couple of weeks, we began our trek. We started out with an entourage of about a half dozen Batad friends. At each place we stopped, a few more joined our group, so by the time we reached the end of our journey, we had a relatively large group of believers with us.

I was constantly reminded of our first experiences of visiting Ifugao villages. Then, they were suspicious of us and avoided interaction with us, but now they welcomed us with open arms. Our routine was to hike in the morning after eating a breakfast of rice or sweet potatoes with vegetables and sometimes a little meat. We usually hiked until midafternoon. By this time, we would be completely exhausted and in need of rest. Usually that was not to be. Just as we kicked off our dusty hiking boots, someone would inevitably sit beside us with the open scriptures and begin.

"About that passage that tells about ... Will you please explain ...?" Others would crowd around, eager to listen to what we might have to say in response.

This would begin a session that would go on all night, with singing, testimonies, and especially reading and explaining the word. Around midnight, Jo and I would be so tired that we would excuse ourselves and sleep. Through the night we would wake up and hear singing or discussion centered on some scripture passage. The next morning we would have breakfast and repeat the procedure again.

One thing that we hadn't really considered was what it would be like without a cushioned place to sit or lie down for three weeks. As the days progressed, the places to sit—usually a log or a stone—became harder and harder, and the places to sleep became almost unbearable. Gradually, as the days and nights passed, every one of our bones that touched the hard places in sitting or sleeping became increasingly sore. Just when we thought we could not endure this harshness any longer, we arrived in Bunhian. The chairs and a bed at the Hilgendorf Clinic for one night was heaven! It was utter luxury! Before we hiked on, we begged and received a square of foam about two inches thick, a foot wide and fully three feet long. This we divided in two, one piece for Jo, and one for me. From then on, we folded these precious pieces and placed them under our hips, which made sleep more bearable again.

By the end of our trip, we had visited fifteen of the thirty-five centers. As a result of our exercise in hiking, Jo had lost ten pounds, and I had lost twelve. We would have preferred that our strenuous exercise happen some other way, but this was a blessing in disguise. We both needed to lose weight.

It was an amazing blessing for us to know that we had been enthusiastically accepted as brother and sister in Christ by our Ifugao Christian friends. More importantly, it was an awesome blessing to know that Ifugao people had embraced the Gospel message that we so dearly loved.

Baptism is a seal of faith for Ifugao Christians, indicating to neighbors and the world that they have forsaken their past life to follow Jesus as their Lord and Savior.

In 1970 nine people were baptized in Batad to form the first church group. By 2000, there were over 125 local churches and perhaps 20,000 Christians throughout Ifugao Province and beyond.

EPILOGUE

The Ifugao Church has continued to grow and develop through the years. When Doreen and I returned home in 1972, there were three churches. In 1977, when Jo and I returned to Ifugao, there were thirty-five churches. Since that time the Ifugao Church has continued to grow. Presently, there are 125 registered churches, with a few still in the formative stage.

A Bible training center was built at the edge of Ifugao where Ifugao Church workers are now being trained to use the Ifugao Bible and assume a major role in the development of the Ifugao Church. Since its inception several years ago, a number of graduates from the two-year program have been ordained pastors of Ifugao churches.

The Ifugao Church became aware that the New Testament that we had translated was only part of God's word—that there was much more not yet translated. They were anxious to have it all, though they probably had no idea how much more there was. More than two-thirds of the scriptures remained to be translated. They decided that they needed the Old Testament as well as the New Testament. They circulated a petition for us to return to translate the Old Testament, but we were already heavily involved in other work. In any event, we felt that they should take the main responsibility for another translation project, and we would help out as much as possible.

After several attempts and failure to get someone from other missions to accept that responsibility, the Ifugao decided to do it themselves. So, Bon'og with the help of a couple of other Ifugao Christians began the long and laborious task. By 2002 Bon'og had completed a rough draft of the entire Old Testament. Two years later he went to be with his Lord, whom he had served so faithfully.

Since that time, other Ifugao young people have been trained and are revising Bon'og's draft. It is now being checked for accuracy and is being prepared for publication. It is to be published, along with a revision of the New Testament, in a single volume within a few years.

978-0-595-40691-3
0-595-40691-2

Printed in the United States
77702LV00003B/100-255